HOW TO SURVIVE THE ABC's
OF LIFE & LEADERSHIP

WHAT TO DO WHEN ACCUSATION, BETRAYAL OR CRISIS COMES YOUR WAY

By

PAUL & JO NAUGHTON

Grosvenor House
Publishing Limited

All rights reserved
Copyright @ Whole Heart Ministries, 2025

The right of Paul & Jo Naughton to be identified as the authors
of this work has been asserted in accordance with Section 78
of the Copyright, Designs and Patents Act 1988

The book cover is copyright to Paul & Jo Naughton

This book is published by
Grosvenor House Publishing Ltd
Link House
140 The Broadway, Tolworth, Surrey, KT6 7HT.
www.grosvenorhousepublishing.co.uk

This book is sold subject to the conditions that it shall not, by way of
trade or otherwise, be lent, resold, hired out or otherwise circulated
without the author's or publisher's prior consent in any form of
binding or cover other than that in which it is published and
without a similar condition including this condition being
imposed on the subsequent purchaser.

A CIP record for this book
is available from the British Library

Paperback ISBN 978-1-83615-074-9
eBook ISBN 978-1-83615-075-6

Some names and details have been changed to protect the
identity of the people whose stories are included in this book.
Bible references are from the New King James Version unless
otherwise stated. The Message and TPT are used to help
reveal the heart of certain passages.

Contents

Part One: Accusation   1

1. The Pain Of Accusation   3
2. Satan's Plan   15
3. God's Purpose   35

Part Two: Betrayal   57

4. The Pain Of Betrayal   59
5. Satan's Plan   67
6. God's Purpose   88

Part Three: Crisis   101

7. The Pain Of Crisis   103
8. Satan's Plan   115
9. God's Purpose   128

Part One
ACCUSATION

"There is one who speaks like the piercings of a sword, but the tongue of the wise promotes health." Proverbs 12:18

Chapter 1

THE PAIN OF ACCUSATION

Scrolling through the comments was like a punch in the guts. One person after another drove their knives into my husband's soul. Some statements were veiled, others were blatant. Within half an hour, about ten people had poured gasoline on a fire and it was burning out of control. After 25 years of faithfully serving a multicultural congregation, Paul was being accused of racial prejudice. It was hard to believe that a man who had spent months of his life ministering across Africa and Asia was being portrayed this way. The accusations pierced my husband's heart. Love it or hate it, social media spreads messages fast and puts them in front of countless strangers at the click of cursor. The algorithms (who gets to see what) are often set to promote the most inflammatory comments. It wasn't long before someone high up in the security services of a foreign nation called my husband. "Too many people have seen this post," he explained, "I am afraid for your safety."

My husband was raised in one of the most violent neighborhoods in London so takes his responsibility for the safety of our family more seriously than most. He has witnessed political groups terrorize victims, attacking both people and property. At the time of these verbal attacks, my husband was already on edge because he had walked through two severe seasons. First, Paul had been interceding through the night for weeks on end as the majority of our church caught Covid in spring 2020 when it was taking many lives. Thankfully, only three of our people were hospitalized and no-one passed away due to the virus. This was an amazing outcome as the death toll around our ministry's location was one of the highest in the world. Our local bus depot lost 11 drivers and eight family members, a friend's church lost 10% of their congregation. The devastation was terrible.

Secondly, our beloved associate pastor and dear friend died after a long battle with cancer. As a result, Paul was exhausted. This unexpected onslaught, together with the menacing words of the foreign security expert, shook my husband to the core. In a matter of days, I watched my powerful protector suffer some sort of emotional meltdown. It is hard enough to see the weak fall apart. It is even more difficult to witness the strong break. I respect my husband more than anyone I have ever met. Watching that incredible man crumble in front of my eyes was heartbreaking. Thank God for His healing power, my husband came out the other side stronger than ever.

Paul's Perspective

Men often react very differently to women to accusation. Some of us internalize the words, we allow them to fester, then suddenly we erupt. When I came under fire, I buried the comments, then my Irish genetic pool stirred me to an angry confrontation. Looking back, I'm sure I responded that way because I received the accusation as rejection. I was wounded, but my pain was hidden behind my anger. But here is the problem with an antagonistic reaction, Proverbs 16:32 (NASB) says, "He who is slow to anger is better than the mighty, and he who rules his spirit, than he who captures a city." Anger weakens us.

We must see accusation as a 'smart' weapon of satan, as an arrow with purpose. If we can figure out the enemy's goal, we can often neutralize his attacks. Our enemy the devil likes to secretly examine our lives to find something that is very dear to our hearts to form the focus of his fiery darts. That way they carry extra venom.

I remember one particular accusation that cut very deep, in fact the words hit me like a punch in the guts. I've always had a passion for financial integrity, taken our giving very seriously, and sought to maintain a pure heart before the Lord. When buying a building for our church, we sacrificially remortgaged our home to help make the purchase possible. A rumor spread that we had bought the building for our own gain, even though a glance at the church records would have revealed the truth. The devil scored a bullseye!

Thankfully I know Jesus as my Wonderful Counsellor. I told Him how much those words hurt, how much my offerings to Him mean to me, then I asked Him to restore my heart, and my love for giving. Thankfully, within weeks I was back cheerfully giving to the Lord and celebrating His abundance.

Has the enemy ever created a 'smart' weapon of accusation against you? It's vital that we learn how to deal with such things. I regularly quote the following scripture over my life: "In righteousness you will be established; you will be far from oppression, for you will not fear; and from terror, for it will not come near you. If anyone fiercely assails you it will not be from Me. Whoever assails you will fall because of you. Behold, I Myself have created the smith who blows the fire of coals And brings out a weapon for its work; and I have created the destroyer to ruin. No weapon that is formed against you will prosper; and every tongue that accuses you in judgment you will condemn. This is the heritage of the servants of the LORD, And their vindication is from Me," declares the LORD." (Isaiah 54:14-17, NASB). It's a great declaration to make over your life too. The enemy may create a smart weapon in an attempt to destroy you, but this Scripture promises that it shall not prosper. It may hit the target, but it will fizzle out and fail.

The Power Of Accusation

Accusation can cut through the soul like a sword pierces flesh. Romans 3:13 (NIV) says, "Their throats are open graves; their tongues practice deceit. The poison of vipers is on their lips."

It's not just what is said, but the way in which it is expressed. It is propelled by judgement and carries blame, often leaving you feeling winded and discredited. It is not just a negative statement, it is charged with anger, and often hatred. We get the word category from the Greek for accuse (katēgoreō) because accusation categorizes you as someone who deserves to be scorned.

The definition of accusation is to bring a charge against someone before a judge. Being convicted in a courtroom requires a due process, whereas accusations are usually leveled with similar force but without the safety of a judicial hearing. Accusation can also make you feel disgraced because exposing statements are broadcast. It can strip you of your dignity and leave you feeling vulnerable. But it does not stop there, it can be intimidating because it sounds threatening. Courtroom accusation leads to punishment if a defendant is found guilty. When words are hurled at you, they often carry the same menacing overtone. I don't know what has been said about you, but I do know that the Lord wants to restore your soul. Time does not heal these wounds, and if they're not dealt with, they can become a source of intimidation long after the words were spoken.

Matthew 7:1 (AMPC) gives clear instructions: "Do not judge and criticize and condemn others, so that you may not be judged and criticized and condemned yourselves..." We are told to avoid accusing others because it is destructive. The enemy will often use criticism to choke your courage and undermine your authority. He wants you to shrink back and doubt yourself, whereas God is ready to restore so that you can arise again. If satan can draw you into a cycle of accusation, negativity and defensiveness, you can end up spiraling out of your destiny and into spiritual mediocrity.

Hebrews 4:15 says, "...we do not have a High Priest who cannot sympathize with our weaknesses, but was in all points tempted as we are, yet without sin." If cruel things have been said about you, Jesus understands the pain. He endured accusation at almost every turn. He healed the sick and was criticized for doing it on the wrong day. His disciples snacked on some wheat, and He was judged for allowing them to work on the sabbath. On one occasion, addressing His accusers, Jesus explained God's heart on the matter: "... I desire mercy..." (Matthew 12:7) God loves to show mercy. His desire is that we would experience His kindness, even when we make mistakes.

Accusation often leads to other problems. Jesus was criticized for healing a withered hand on the Sabbath. Scripture says what happened next: "Then the Pharisees went out and plotted against Him, how they might destroy Him." (Matthew 12:14). First, they accused Him, then they sought to kill Him. Every accusation has a purpose; the enemy wants to use harsh judgements to derail God's plans for your life. That's why we need to dismantle accusation's power in our lives.

Matthew 11:18-19 shows the futility of judgement: "For John came neither eating nor drinking, and they say, 'He has a demon.' The Son of Man came eating and drinking, and they say, 'Look, a glutton and a winebibber, a friend of tax collectors and sinners!' ..." You can't win when it comes to people's approval, so please don't try. Ask the Lord to heal your heart any time you are sharply criticized but accept that you will face it again.

The Ultimate Accuser

The devil is the puppet master that incites accusation. Revelation 12:10b (NASB) says, "...the accuser of our brethren has been thrown down, he who accuses them before our God day and night." It's not just that satan occasionally makes charges against believers, it is his full-time job. He is the accuser, and he is constantly looking for opportunities to accuse you of falling short. He wants you to give up and he knows that accusation can help him accomplish his dirty work. You and I should never throw allegations against our brothers or sisters. That job is already taken.

The dictionary definition of accusation is 'an allegation that a person is guilty of some fault, offense or crime'. The truth is that you have probably had many accusations hurled at you at home in the heat of disagreements, at work during a disagreement, or even at church. Even when they are said out of anger rather than intention, they can hurt terribly. Perhaps your spouse blamed you for your marital problems. Maybe your brother or sister held you responsible for their suffering. Your friend could have criticized the way you handled a difficult situation. It may be more mundane. Whatever happened, judgement hurts. Not only that, the words can also get lodged in your soul.

The Power Of Words

Words can be lethal weapons. Proverbs 12:18 says, "There is one who speaks like the piercings of a sword..." This verse exposes the violence of accusation. It can feel like a stab in your heart. If the words are spoken by someone you love or trust, the pain can run deep. Maybe you have been accused of corruption or cruelty. Perhaps you have been told that your heart is crooked or that your motives were twisted. It could be more specific. Whatever complaints have been made about you, I imagine that you have been hurt, your confidence may also have been knocked. I want you to know that God is ready to heal your heart.

Proverbs 18:21 tells us that, "Death and life are in the power of the tongue..." The Message Translation puts it this way: "Words kill, words give life; they're either poison or fruit..." (Proverbs 18:21 MSG) Please don't underestimate the harmful effects of angry words. If you had been stabbed in the chest, you would rush to the emergency room for immediate treatment. In the same way, your soul needs to be restored after verbal attacks. The starting point is acknowledging the pain and your need to be healed.

You probably know about of the armor of God. Ephesians 6 describes heavenly clothing that is designed to protect you from demonic attacks. One protective armory that we need is the shield of faith. In Ephesians 6:16, we are instructed to take up: "... the shield of faith with which you will be able to quench all the fiery darts of the wicked one." The Greek word for fiery means to be inflamed with anger or grief. Fiery darts are words charged with rage. Darts are arrows that are thrown with force to ensure that they pierce. I believe that fiery darts are a demonic plot to wound those that God has called.

Isn't Accusation Evaluation?

The motive behind feedback is usually the desire to bring improvement and change. The motive behind accusation is usually the desire to expose or hurt. Of course, the Lord wants us to be aware of our shortcomings so that we can grow. However, accusation makes it almost impossible to evaluate yourself correctly. Mixing aggression with feedback can come across as an attack, so our instinctive reaction is often defense. If you have been accused of anything, you'll know it hurts. If those that were pointing the finger were people you loved, the wound will probably be deep. During a time of intense public accusation, I remember falling on my kitchen floor, "This is awful!" I cried out to the Lord, "It hurts so much to have our actions and motives pulled apart."

King David knew the pain of accusing words. In Psalms 41:5-7 (NLT), he wrote, "But my enemies say nothing but evil about me. "How soon will he die and be forgotten?" They visit me as if they were my friends, but all the while they gather gossip, and when they leave, they spread it everywhere. All who hate me whisper about me, imagining the worst." Slanderous statements defile a person. The Greek word for slander means evil speaking which damages another's good name. If lies have been told about you or if you have been vilified, it will probably have made you feel smeared. It's difficult to run your race if you're feeling ashamed. Jesus paid the price for all your shortcomings and failures; He does not want you to be blamed for sin He has already carried on the cross.

Being Under Suspicion

God's original plan was that we would all live in an affirming atmosphere where people believe the best. God is love and His desire is for you to be surrounded by love. 1 Corinthians 13:7 (AMP) says, "Love… is ever ready to believe the best of every person, its hopes are fadeless under all circumstances, and it endures everything [without weakening]." When you are surrounded by trust and confidence, it enables you to become your best. In contrast, when you are viewed with suspicion, it can be debilitating and may lead to anxiety. When others doubt you, all too often you end up doubting yourself.

You may feel as though every step you take is under the spotlight. We all make mistakes. However, when you are being scrutinized, even small mess-ups can feel like major falls. When you're in leadership, your life is on show. People often think that they have the right to cross-examine every word you speak or every step you take. When the enemy comes in through character attacks, it can feel as though everything you do is open to misunderstanding.

Leaders examined Jesus' every move, trying to trip Him up. Their accusations were intended to destroy His reputation and diminish His influence. Mark 3:2 says, "So they watched Him closely, whether He would heal him on the Sabbath, so that they might accuse Him." The Pharisees (who had six days a week to heal the guy) were trying to trap Jesus like a predator closing in on its prey (see Mark 3:6). Perhaps you have been in a situation like that. I want you to know that you are by no means alone, your Wonderful Counsellor understands your pain.

As we already saw, David is another giant of faith who knew what it was like to have his daily life cross examined. 1 Samuel 18:8-9 says, "Then Saul was very angry, and the saying displeased him; and he said, "They have ascribed to David ten thousands, and to me they have ascribed only thousands. Now what more can he have but the kingdom?" So, Saul eyed David from that day forward."

David didn't do anything to hurt the king or his kingdom, but Saul watched the young warrior with suspicion from that day onwards. The king told his soldiers that David was a traitor. Saul instructed armies that once followed David into battle to kill him. Imagine how he must have felt knowing that his former boss and spiritual father now hated his guts and wanted him dead.

Innocent Until Proven Guilty

The UK justice system states that a person is innocent until proven guilty. This is love's way too (see 1 Corinthians 13:7 AMP). Suspicion, on the other hand, says that you are guilty until proven innocent. It creates a burden that is too heavy for most to carry. It demands that you justify your every move. Suspicion is never satisfied with a simple explanation. It digs for dirt and blames. It is exhausting and can strip even strong men and women of courage. That's what the devil wants.

Let's look again at Psalms 41:5-7 (AMP) when David told the Lord about his pain: "My enemies speak evil of me, [saying], When will he die and his name perish? And when one comes to see me, he speaks falsehood and empty words, while his heart gathers mischievous gossip [against me]; when he goes away, he tells it abroad. All who hate me whisper together about me; against me do they devise my hurt [imagining the worst for me]." These people were hellbent on destroying David. They constantly searched for evidence against the man after God's own heart (see Acts 13:22). David was far from perfect, but he was quick to put things right when he got things wrong. However, the people around him tore him apart. He must have felt like he was living on a knife's edge, afraid of taking a wrong step. This is how sustained periods of accusation can feel.

Twisting Words

Have people twisted your words? Have they taken what you said and made it sound as though you said something different. If so, you're not alone. Speaking of His death, Jesus said in John 2:19b, "... Destroy this temple, and in three days I will raise it up." The religious leaders twisted His words and used them to accuse Him of blasphemy in Matthew 26:61: "This fellow said, 'I am able to destroy the temple of God and to build it in three days.'" Jesus never said that He would destroy the temple. He said something that *sounded* similar but was very different. Often accusations are convincing because although they are false, they resemble the truth.

Sometimes accusations tell half a story and misconstrue the heart of the person under fire. This can cause even loyal friends to question the motives or behavior of someone they know. Words are seeds, so they have the capability of producing a harvest in the heart of the hearer. Words influence opinions and attitudes. They can alter perceptions. That's why Jesus warned us to be guarded in Luke 8:18a (NASB), "So take care how you listen..." Accusations can make people who once loved you, doubt you. Others may become suspicious about your motives.

If you have experienced the pain of accusation, it is important that you are healed. We will pray together at the end of this chapter. Remember that Jesus understands. He was accused privately and publicly, He was accused by His nearest and dearest, as well as by well-known leaders. His close friend Judas alleged that Jesus mishandled the ministry's finances. The leaders in Jerusalem claimed He disobeyed the Word of God. Jesus was accused of conspiring to destroy a public building. Well known personalities lied about His actions and His motives. He was mocked and He was hated. Jesus has walked the road you have travelled, and He wants to heal you anywhere you hurt.

Another man that had his words and motives twisted by critics was Stephen. The leaders of his day became jealous of the attention that he was receiving and resented the impact that his preaching was having on people. Acts 6:11 describes their role in whipping up anger towards Stephen: "Then they secretly induced men to say, "We have heard him speak blasphemous words against Moses and God." Stephen was stoned to death by an angry crowd who believed accusations that could not have been further from the truth.

Secondhand Hurts

When my husband came under accusation, my all-time low was probably the evening I lay beside Paul in bed while his heart pounded out of his chest uncontrollably. I did not know if my husband would make it through the night. Watching a loved one come under attack can be heartbreaking. Maybe you have witnessed someone crumble under the weight of criticism. Despite your desire to support them, you may have felt helpless. Perhaps you were adversely affected by the fallout.

Jeremiah knew what it was like to be pained by the agony of others. He wrote in Jeremiah 8:21, "For the hurt of the daughter of my people I am hurt. I am mourning; astonishment has taken hold of me." If you have been saddened watching someone you love suffer, God wants to restore your soul. Secondhand trauma can be unexpectedly difficult to bear. Your Heavenly Father does not want you to dismiss your pain simply because someone else went through more. If it hurt you, the Lord wants to heal you. We can learn from airplane safety announcements: "Please fix your own mask before helping anyone else with theirs." When you have been restored, you will be in a much better place to support your loved one. Many times, witnessing your healing journey causes them to seek their own.

Malice

The book of Acts devotes a chapter to an accusation brought by a public speaker called Tertullus against Paul the Apostle. Paul's accuser began by flattering the judge. Acts 24:2-3 says, "... through you we enjoy great peace, and prosperity is being brought to this nation by your foresight ...most noble Felix..." It is common for accusers to flatter the people with whom they are sharing their derogatory stories. Flattery is a foul counterfeit of encouragement. Encouragement is focused on others and is designed to build confidence. Flattery is self-serving and is used to secure support. Tertullus complemented the judge to win his favor and get him on side. Afterwards, he laid into Paul.

Paul's accuser publicly declared in Acts 24:5, "We have found this man a plague, a creator of dissension among all the Jews throughout the world, and a ringleader of the sect of the Nazarenes." Tertullus called Paul a plague. The Greek word loimos which is used in the original text of this verse means a disease. He was trying to ruin Paul's reputation by assassinating his character. Because good character gives you the right to speak into the lives of others, the enemy will always attempt to undermine your integrity. If anyone has condemned you with their words, lied about you, or twisted the truth to make you seem corrupt, God wants to restore your soul, and your reputation. Let's pray.

Heavenly Father,

I open up my heart to You. I ask You to reveal any damage caused by accusation over the course of my life. Uncover buried pain that has affected my outlook or my decisions. I want to be free to fulfill every ounce of my potential, so I ask You to shine Your light into the depths of my heart and highlight any hidden issues. Expose any wounds in my soul and heal me deep within. (*Now talk to the Lord about any words that have come to mind. Tell Him what was said and how it affected you. Talk to the Lord about what you went through, share your story with Him in as much detail as possible.*) I ask You to begin healing my heart, Lord. I give You my pain and I ask You to fill me afresh with Your healing love. As I read this book, Lord, I ask You to take me on a journey to liberty and healing.

In Jesus' name I pray,

Amen.

Chapter 2

SATAN'S PLAN

Accusation causes so much damage that the devil has taken on accusing God's people as a full-time job. Let's look again at Revelation 12:10b: "... the accuser of our brethren, who accused them before our God day and night..." Although he is wicked, satan is not stupid. The fact that he spends so much of his time accusing believers demonstrates how badly accusation can injure people. If the wounds are left unchecked, they can end up distorting your view of yourself and your entire outlook. Understanding sheds light and paves the way to restoration. I will now look at some of the most common consequences of verbal attacks.

1. Pain

A knife attack can be fatal. If you have ever been stabbed, I am sure you sought immediate medical help. I have never been assaulted so I can only imagine the shock and pain. Proverbs 12:18a says, 'There is one who speaks like the piercings of a sword..." According to scripture, accusation is an assault. The stabbing can come with such force that it knocks the life out of you. Talking to the Lord, King David said in Psalms 64:3 (NLT): "They sharpen their tongues like swords and aim their bitter words like arrows." David compared angry words with swords and arrows. He saw accusations thrown at him as vicious weapons intended to wound.

Culture has taught a cruel lie. Children in playgrounds across the world repeat myths like: "Sticks and stones may break my bones, but words will never hurt me." I wish this were so, but it is far from the truth. Accusation can tear you apart. It can squash your confidence and make you feel ashamed. Words can dash dreams and terminate destiny relationships. Make no mistake, words are powerful. They can breathe life and build bright futures, but they can also devastate their victims.

Sometimes, accusations focus on your failures, at other times, they question you, your gifts, or the decisions you make. Paul the apostle suffered many character attacks. He was often belittled, even by believers. 2 Corinthians 10:10 describes one such example: "For his letters," they say, "are weighty and powerful, but his bodily presence is weak, and his speech contemptible." Some at the church in Corinth mocked Paul's speech impediment, suggesting he was an inadequate minister of the gospel. They accused him of being powerful in writing, yet pathetic in person. Paul had poured out his life into the lives of those who were putting him down.

Most people seek help when they are physically sick, but a broken bone is less serious than a broken spirit. Proverbs 18:14 says, "The spirit of a man will sustain him in sickness, but who can bear a broken spirit?" Please don't disregard the damage that angry words can do to your heart. You would know what to do if your arm or leg were fractured, but do you know how to respond when cruel comments have been hurled your way? It starts by acknowledging the pain so that you can begin to heal.

If you have been accused of wrongdoing by friends or family, it's time to admit how much it hurt. Instead of hiding from the allegations or trying to ignore the attack, stop and ask yourself how the words made you feel. Denying that you were wounded will not make your pain go away, you need to be healed. Stop for a moment before we go any further and ask the Lord to search your heart for any wounds left behind by hurtful words. Asking the Lord to unearth any accusations that may have unknowingly influenced your life or behavior could lead you to some life changing encounters in His presence.

Bitter Words

One time while I was worshiping, the Lord interrupted my song to tell me that I needed to uproot bitterness. I was surprised; I had worked overtime to fully forgive people involved in a particularly painful season. Immediately after the Lord spoke, certain phrases began replaying in my heart. The Holy Spirit then showed me that words were lodged deep down. God took me to four statements that still made me feel very uncomfortable. I often heard these phrases play out in my thoughts. I realized that I needed to deal with these arrows.

One by one, I told the Lord what was said and why it hurt me. I described the pain that I felt while I prayed. I shared how wrong it felt. I cried as I poured out my heart like water before the face of the Lord (see Lamentations 2:19). I hadn't even realized that those comments had cut me to the core. After sharing my pain with my Wonderful Counsellor (see Isaiah 9:6), I forgave the people who said those things. I cancelled any debt that I felt they owed me, and I asked the Lord to bless them. Afterwards, my heart felt free. Within a short while of my healing, I could not even remember the comments! Words that had once been engraved in my mind were erased. Remember, until the Holy Spirit spoke to me, I had no idea that these words were lodged in my soul.

Psalms 64:3 says: "Who sharpen their tongue like a sword, and bend their bows to shoot their arrows – bitter words." Sometimes unjust words can get imbedded in the hidden caverns of your heart. Long after they have been said, they may still be able to disturb your peace. Psalms 140:3 (NLT) describes the intensity of such attacks: "Their tongues sting like a snake; the venom of a viper drips from their lips." The Lord wants to heal the pain, cleanse away any angst left behind, and restore your confidence. If you vividly recall any unkind or unjust comments, go back to those experiences with the Holy Spirit by your side. Tell your Wonderful Counsellor how you felt and ask the Lord to remove the fiery darts from your heart.

2. Shame

Several years ago, during a leadership meeting, a church overseer accused my husband and me of rebellion and threatened to have us removed. To say that we were blind-sided is an understatement. I felt like someone had ripped out my insides. Unable to sleep the night it happened, the Lord reminded me of Proverbs 18:14 (NIV): "The human spirit can endure in sickness, but a crushed spirit who can bear?" Some experiences are so distressing that they can break you. You may feel winded or find yourself reeling from the shock. I felt like the life had been kicked out of me that awful evening.

Prompted by the Spirit, I got out of bed in the middle of the night and went to my prayer closet where I burst into uncontrollable tears. Sharing my shock in prayer, I released pent up anguish. I asked the Lord to heal my heart then rested for a while in His presence. I woke up the following morning at peace. Although the Lord healed the bruising of that first meeting, that was just the start of three months of distress. Rumors about us spread in church circles but the Lord instructed us to say nothing. He told us that He would vindicate, and we must not attempt to clear our names. During this time, people who were once friends distanced themselves. As my husband and I walked into church services, people would look the other way. I felt tainted by the accusations.

I Want To Hide

Ever since the Garden of Eden, human reactions to shame have remained the same. Adam and Eve hid themselves and then they covered their nakedness. Genesis 3:7 says, "...they knew that they were naked; and they sewed fig leaves together and made themselves coverings." The sense of exposure that shame brings makes us want to cover up or look away. Facing feelings of shame can be intensely uncomfortable. Adam and Eve also tried to hide themselves from the Lord. They could not bear the burden of guilt nor their moral failure. Let me stop for a minute. If you have missed the mark, the enemy may be telling you that it's over. He could be trying to convince you that you have no way out. That is a lie. Please do not run away from your Heavenly Father. Run to Him. He has a plan for your restoration. Shame also causes us to gloss over how we really feel because facing feelings of shame is intensely unpleasant.

Wanting to hide is a problem. In Mark 4:21b (NLT), Jesus asked a rhetorical question, "Would anyone light a lamp and then put it under a basket or under a bed? Of course not! A lamp is placed on a stand, where its light will shine." Jesus is the light of the world (see John 8:12). When you invite Him into your life, you invite His light into your life too. God's desire is that the brightness of His presence will be visible in you. Shame is one way that the devil tries to hide Christ.

I will never forget a word from the Lord that my husband once released at our church: "My gifts are trapped in the hearts of My people." God gives gifts to every single one of His children. Ephesians 4:16 (NLT) says, "He makes the whole body fit together perfectly. As each part does its own special work, it helps the other parts grow, so that the whole body is healthy and growing and full of love." You have gifts that will help others.

Once God gives you supernatural abilities, He will not take them back. Romans 11:29 explains that "...the gifts and the calling of God are irrevocable." Your Heavenly Father will not change His mind about your purpose. When you feel smeared by accusations, it can make you want to hide. But when you hide, your gifts become inactive. They lose expression. Those gifts were not given to you for you to keep to yourself, they are for you to share with the people around you. Perhaps you are a gifted leader or a wonderful encourager. You could be an anointed teacher or a powerful prayer warrior. Shame wants you to retreat and when you do, God's gifts in you get trapped.

Disgust

All too often, an accuser has a tone of disgust in their voice. Disgust communicates filth and loathing; it can make a person feel dirty. King David's wife was disgusted at him on one occasion and hurled abuse at him. Let's look at 2 Samuel 6:20 (NLT): "When David returned home to bless his own family, Michal, the daughter of Saul, came out to meet him. She said in disgust, "How distinguished the king of Israel looked today, shamelessly exposing himself to the servant girls like any vulgar person might do!" These words were intended to make David feel repulsive so that he would change his behavior.

Maybe someone close to you has muddied your reputation with their words of disgust. Perhaps the damage done was to your heart rather than your image. Either way, you may feel tarnished. The enemy wants to use such attacks to stop you from stepping out. He wants you to draw back. I can't tell you how many times I have felt like slowing down when people have sharply criticized me or the ministry. If someone threw mud at you, you would feel dirty. When words of disgust are hurled at you, it can have a similar impact. It can also make you feel disqualified or doubt your right to serve. This is satan's goal.

Jesus understands public disgust. In Mark 9:12, He talked about the attacks He was about to endure: "… the Son of Man… must suffer many things and be treated with contempt" The Greek for contempt (exoudenoō) means to make utterly nothing of, to despise. The enemy wants you to be despised because he knows the impact that hatred can have. It can make you feel worthless, as though you are nothing. If things have been said or done that stripped a sense of dignity from you, your Heavenly Father wants to heal your heart.

A Different Version Of Events

Shame is so distressing that it can be hard to acknowledge the way it makes us feel. Let me paint a picture to help you understand. Imagine a talented high school student giving a public presentation for the first time. We will call this young man Phil. A confident teenager, Phil is a great communicator who is looking forward to giving a speech at school. However, as Phil steps onto the platform, let's imagine that he trips in front of the entire school, much to the hilarity of his fellow students.

Feeling devastated, Phil would probably pull himself together, hurry his way through his speech and then exit at his earliest opportunity. Asked afterwards by his parents how it went, I could imagine Phil saying, "It was okay, but I don't think public speaking is for me after all." Telling his parents about the fall and how awful he felt would probably be too uncomfortable. He might not even face the truth himself. Instead, Phil would cover up his feelings and invent a different version of reality. In one five second trip, shame could cause a young person to close a promising door of opportunity.

If allegations have been made against you, or your reputation muddied, you may feel humiliated. You may want to take a step back or even throw in the towel. Perhaps you have listened to that inner voice trying to convince you that you weren't cut out for ministry or 'this type of work' after all. The enemy wants you to hide. But remember, you are not alone. Joseph was accused of rape, King David was accused of murder, the apostle Paul was accused of inciting riots, and Jesus was accused of blasphemy. Accusation is part of life. Instead of hiding or listening to a false narrative, ask the Lord to heal your heart of every wound, ask Him to cleanse you of all shame.

In my book, The Many Faces Of Shame, I lead readers on a journey to healing and freedom. I highlight several steps to freedom from shame including facing the truth about the way you feel, sharing the pain of shame in prayer, asking the Lord to cleanse your heart, and rising up again in the knowledge that you are clothed with honor by God. If you feel like shame has kept you bound, I wholeheartedly recommend this book to you for further study and healing. It's the devil's plan that you feel smeared, but Jesus made the way for you to rise up strong.

3. Guilt & Condemnation

There may be an element of truth woven into an accusation, and as a result, the words can make you feel condemned. You may think that you have no right to be hurt. You could blame yourself. It's important to remember that the blood of Jesus has the power to silence every argument against you. 1 John 1:9 is clear, "If we confess our sins, He is faithful and just to forgive us our sins and to cleanse us from all unrighteousness." When you repent, the Lord forgives you and wipes away every trace of guilt. People may say you are guilty, but God says you are free. You may need to forgive yourself.

After you have been forgiven, God goes a step further. Colossians 2:14 (NLT) says, "He canceled the record of the charges against us and took it away by nailing it to the cross." Not only are you pronounced innocent, but every record of wrong is blotted out and every argument against you is dismantled. People may try to make you pay for past mistakes, but before God, you are righteous. Folk may try to muddy your reputation by exposing old errors, but you stand clean before the King of Kings.

God cannot mix with unrighteousness. Being reconciled with Him is powerful. It detaches you from every trace of sin and unites you with His perfect nature. Colossians 1:22 (NLT) is clear: "Yet now he has reconciled you to himself through the death of Christ in his physical body. As a result, he has brought you into his own presence, and you are holy and blameless as you stand before him without a single fault." Thanks to the blood of Jesus, you stand before the God of heaven and earth blameless. God counts you unblemished by past mistakes and faultless before Him.

Accusation Versus Conviction

Accusation is the devil's counterfeit of conviction. Conviction is motivated by love and its purpose is to bring restoration. Accusation is motivated by anger and is designed to cause condemnation. The devil accuses. The Spirit of God convicts. As long as we don't resist the conviction of the Holy Spirit, as long as we don't cover up when we mess up, we can be restored to righteousness after falling. Proverbs 24:16 (NIV) is clear: "For though the righteous fall seven times, they rise again..." Jesus paid the price for our restoration to righteousness every time we fall.

Romans 8 begins with a famous verse, but before I share that Scripture, I want to look at the topic of the previous chapter. Romans 7 reflects on the constant battle every believer fights with the flesh nature. "For I fail to practice the good deeds I desire to do, but the evil deeds that I do not desire to do are what I am [ever] doing." (Romans 7:19 AMP) The writer to the church at Rome expresses the difficulty of overcoming the sinful nature. The entire chapter describes the struggle Christians face on their walk to holiness. It is immediately after that chapter that Romans 8:1-2 (NLT) declares, "So now there is no condemnation for those who belong to Christ Jesus. And because you belong to him, the power of the life-giving Spirit has freed you from the power of sin that leads to death." God does not condemn you – you are His child.

4. Self-Doubt

We looked earlier at the fact that sometimes the things said may have been factual. On other occasions, you might have been lied about. The thing about accusation is that, factual or false, it can erode your confidence. On eight separate occasions Joshua was commanded in Scripture to: "Be strong and of good courage"

(Deuteronomy 31:6, Deuteronomy 31:7, Deuteronomy 31:23, Joshua 1:6, Joshua 1:7, Joshua 1:9, Joshua 1:18). Joshua had a crucial yet challenging leadership role. Faintheartedness was therefore not an option. You too have a vital part to play so it is crucial that you are confident. No-one else is equipped to fulfill your purpose, in fact, you were called to the kingdom for such a time as this (see Esther 4:14). God wants you to be bold and strong so that you will fulfill every ounce of your God given potential.

Self-doubt is a horrible side effect of accusation. If the devil can make you feel disqualified, you will question your authority – and perhaps even your identity as a minister or leader. Allegations may make you wonder if you still have the right to serve God. I want you to know that this is the devil's plan. He wants to squash your confidence so that you won't use your gifts. He wants you to shrink back so that your anointing is trapped behind closed doors. Please remember the story of Moses. He ran away after killing an Egyptian, then argued with God about his ability, delaying the departure of Israel from Egypt by thirty years.

When self-doubt enters a person's heart, courage evaporates. The enemy knows the power of righteous people: "... the righteous are bold as a lion" (Proverbs 28:1b) so he tries to make you doubt your standing before Christ. Courageous people pursue their purpose, even when it is painful. Brave men and women share Jesus with the world and stand up for what they believe. The enemy wants you to question yourself because he wants your confidence to crumble. In contrast, Philemon 6 instructs you to focus on the good that God has placed inside you.

Hebrews 10:35-36 explains the importance of self-belief: "Therefore do not cast away your confidence, which has great reward. For you have need of endurance, so that after you have done the will of God, you may receive the promise." Confidence enables you to pursue your purpose with perseverance. It is essential that you allow the Lord to heal the wounds of every accusation that has been leveled against you so that you can boldly arise again.

5. Shrinking Back

Accusation has power. Of course, the words wound and the intent hurts. However, there is more to it than that. When accusations come from people we love or admire, or someone in some sort of authority, they can constrain us. They may have been said once, but you may hear them repeatedly in your mind. Even seemingly unimportant complaints could have you questioning your calling. I want to share a trivial but personal example of how words can hold us back.

Sometime back, my husband and I went through a very painful season. I had unwittingly wounded him in a way that took him back to the first decade of our marriage when I constantly rejected his affections. My actions one morning hurt him badly. When we were discussing the incident in the days afterwards, he made this statement, "You dress up to minister for your social media stuff, but when do you dress up for your husband?"

These unremarkable words threw me. Because we were going through a painful season, I was raw and sensitive. I kept thinking about his words, and although I suspected he didn't mean what he had said, I was floored. Having been doing social media broadcasts weekly for two or three years, I stopped for about three weeks. His comment made me feel like I had no right to minister through this medium. When I eventually started again (because I knew I had to be obedient), I wore little makeup. I struggled.

Sometimes small wounds are debilitating. Please don't dismiss comments that hurt just because you think you should have been more resilient. If the words hurt, you need to be healed to ensure you are free to follow Jesus. Song of Songs 2:15 says, "Catch us the foxes, the little foxes that spoil the vines, for our vines have tender grapes." Often the enemy uses little issues to try to take you off course because he knows you are likely to dismiss their significance.

We know from Romans 8:14 that, "... as many as are led by the Spirit of God, these are sons of God." Part of being a mature child of God is following the leading of His Spirit. This is one reason why buried pain is dangerous. Until we deal with hidden hurts, they have a habit of controlling our decisions. Even if you do the right thing, your attitude is also important to the Lord. Colossians 3:23 is clear, "And whatever you do, do it heartily, as to the Lord and not to men." I had to be healed of my husband's throwaway comment so that I could obey God from my heart. Reluctance to do what's right is often an indicator of an unresolved wound.

6. Fear and Intimidation

During a period of accusations against my husband and me, I became increasingly intimidated. After everything calmed down, I found myself suffering from anxiety. Even the slightest reminder of the season we walked through sent me into a spin. News items on related topics, passing references in conversations, or mention of the people involved would cause instant emotional reactions. My stomach would knot up and my heart would race. Residual distress would spring to the surface and steal my peace. I had broken fear's power over my life years earlier, or so I thought. I no longer worried what people thought of me, but I was easily intimidated by overbearing or domineering people.

Deep Recesses Of The Soul

I tried rebuking fear and casting off my cares about the future as we are instructed in 1 Peter 5:7, but that was only part of the problem. Shock and pain were trapped in my soul. I realized that two events during that period had traumatized me. I could not get rid of the anxiety until the pain was gone. And I could not get rid of the pain until I went back to those memories. I got into God's presence and told my Heavenly Father how much it had hurt to see my husband break into pieces. As I prayed, I told the Lord how scared I was on the night when I could feel my husband's heart pounding out of his chest. I told my Wonderful Counselor how tense and upsetting the home atmosphere was in that season.

It wasn't just the effect on my husband that hurt. Although our son was away, our beautiful daughter went through the whole trauma. She has a sensitive spirit and dislikes conflict. This period therefore took a toll on her. On several occasions, she broke down as we talked. It made me sad to see this hurting her so much. I poured this pain out before the Lord and He healed my heart. After the healing flowed, my strength returned, and I took authority over the spirit of intimidation. It wasn't long before I was back to normal. Words that once triggered anxiety now passed by unnoticed. Faces that had caused concern now provoked compassion. The way we know that we are free is that the memories that once produced negative reactions lose their power.

Bullying Talk

1 Kings 19:1-2 exposes one way that intimidation worms its way into our lives: "And Ahab told Jezebel all that Elijah had done, also how he had executed all the prophets with the sword. Then Jezebel sent a messenger to Elijah, saying, "So let the gods do to me, and more also, if I do not make your life as the life of one of them by tomorrow about this time." Ahab talked to Jezebel, the biggest bully in Israel, about Elijah. The king told his wife what Elijah had done in order to stir up trouble for the Prophet. The enemy uses offense and outrage to get people talking about each other. The devil knows that if he can draw us into slandering other believers, he can pour gasoline on volatile situations.

Proverbs 26:20-23 says, "Where there is no wood, the fire goes out and where there is no gossip, strife ceases. As charcoal is to burning coals, and wood to fire, so is a contentious man to kindle strife. The words of a talebearer are like tasty trifles, and they go down into the inmost body. Fervent lips with a wicked heart are like earthenware covered with silver dross." The word used for wicked in verse 23 also means grievous or troublesome. Someone who is grieved and forcefully sharing their troubles creates problems. We all know the tone used when conversations are dripping with accusations. It is the enemy's ideal atmosphere.

If you have come under attack, with people tearing you apart behind your back, then you will probably have felt the threats of the spirit of intimidation. Remember, our primary struggle is never against flesh and blood (see Ephesians 6:12), even though the enemy uses people. Perhaps family or former friends have discussed your flaws. Maybe your choices have been called into question. The devil wants you to be afraid of what people might be saying. In truth, you will never actually know what is being said about you by others behind closed doors. Listening to your negative imaginations is therefore counterproductive.

The spirit of intimidation, on the other hand, is very real. You cannot conquer any enemy by running away. Goliath was probably twice the size of David who was just a teenager. Nevertheless, when the giant approached the shepherd boy, David ran towards Goliath (see 1 Samuel 17:48). In the same way, it is vital that you face your fears. Look directly at the issues that cause intimidation. Ask God to heal any pain that personal attacks caused and then rebuke the enemy. We will share the way to healing and freedom in the next chapter.

7. Hatred

Accusation can make you feel hated. That's one of the reasons it can feel so brutal. Hatred is the absolute opposite of love, and just as unconditional love overflows from our Heavenly Father, so hatred spews straight from satan. I went to college when I was nineteen years of age. Full of zeal for the Lord, I was determined to share my faith with fellow students. About three weeks after I moved into university accommodation, I found myself at the center of a heated discussion about abortion. I shared my belief that life begins at conception and that it is sacred. Before I knew it,

I was surrounded by nine or ten students pointing at me and yelling. "You're a foul bigot," one shouted. "You think you're above the rest of us," another announced. Their angry accusations were fired one after another. I was shocked into silence. Eventually, the crowd scattered, and I was left alone.

The force with which each charge was made winded me. Shock entered and a fear of experiencing anything like that again gripped my heart. I believe that attack was a door opener to me backsliding. I became afraid of being attacked for my faith, so I tempered my zeal for the Lord. Being liked by my peers became a goal so I joined their parties and drifted away from Christian meetings. When hatred is unleashed, it is awful. It can feel like being beaten. If you have come under fire and felt the force of hatred, God wants to heal your heart.

David knew hatred's cruelty. In Psalms 9:13 he cried out, "Have mercy on me, O Lord! Consider my trouble from those who hate me..." God knows the distress that being despised can cause. The word used here for trouble is ăniy and it means depression and misery. Hatred can even cause depression. You were made in the image of God, and God is love. His original plan was that you would live in an atmosphere of kindness. It is therefore not surprising that hatred hurts. If you have felt the pain of being despised, the Lord wants to heal your heart.

Don't Take The Bait

Being accused is not only painful, but also wrong. The sense of injustice that arises inside can be almost overwhelming. Remember, the devil always has plans for your pain. He wants to use the injustice of your suffering to get you offended. Satan wants to constantly remind you about the wrong you suffered so he will try to surround you with people who talk about the outrage.

Job 4:12-13 explains how thoughts take root: "Now a word was secretly brought to me, and my ear received a whisper of it.

In disquieting thoughts from the visions..." Indignation is usually shared behind closed doors – secretly. If you listen to those words, they soon take root in your heart. Before you know it, you have taken satan's bait. If you've been a Christian for a while, you will have heard lots of teaching on offense. The danger is that you assume you're *not* offended. 'I'm just upset,' you may say, or 'it's not my issue, it's all their doing.' Offense tries to hide. While we deny it's there, we can remain bound. When we call it what it is and deal with it, we are on our way to freedom. Here are some of the signs...

Offense shakes its head at the wrongs of others. It shares what happened with friends or family. It rehearses the events of the past, often imagining how it would address the perpetrator if they were to meet. Any time offense pictures the face of the person who hurt him, he feels a hardening in his heart. Offense resents it when the one who wronged him succeeds. Offense is like a splinter. It might be small, but until it is removed, it will cause irritation and could get infected. Left unchecked, offense can derail your destiny.

Jesus warned us about the dangers of offense in the parable of the sower. In Mark 4:17b (AMP), Jesus said: "... when trouble or persecution arises on account of the Word, they immediately are offended (become displeased, indignant, resentful) and they stumble and fall away." We are called to run the race set before us (see 1 Corinthians 9:24) which means pursuing our purpose with vigor. Offense takes our eyes off our God given goals and causes us to stumble.

Forgiveness is a powerful, spiritual antibiotic! It cleans out even the deepest wound so that you can heal without any lasting problems. It sets you free from the people who have caused you pain. The best way I know to assess whether you have fully forgiven is by using what I call, 'The Smile Test'. Close your eyes and picture the face of the person who wounded you. How do you feel when you see them in your mind's eye? Do any negative emotions stir inside? Can you smile from your heart at their image? If you don't pass the smile test, you still need to forgive.

Undermining Destiny

It never occurred to me that the message I am called to preach would make anyone angry. However, when you declare that there is no trauma or tragedy that God cannot completely heal, you unwittingly challenge anyone who does not want to embrace total restoration. Healing demands laying down self-pity, a victim mindset and every argument that expects special concessions from others.

The ministry that I thought the world would love started to attract some attack. However, the attack was of course leveled at the messenger rather than the message. The first accusation was that I claim to bring healing, when really, I am hurting others. Then my motives for carrying restoration were questioned. Every minister gets criticized, but I didn't think the restoration message would be knocked. It felt as though my accusers were throwing mud at a precious work that is transforming lives. I was floored by the charges, and, for the first time ever, I felt self-conscious about my calling.

The devil will always target you in the area of your destiny. He does not care if you are a nice Christian. He hates it when you fulfill your God-given purpose. His aim is to take you out of your lane and steal God's Word out of your life. He wants to prevent you from doing what the Lord designed *you* to do. I brought the things people said to the Lord in prayer. I shared the shock of such an attack in God's presence and told my Wonderful Counsellor how much these accusations hurt. The Lord healed my heart, but I also had to become more resilient. I had to learn to reject negativity *before* it entered my soul.

Ecclesiastes 7:21 says, "Also do not take to heart everything people say, lest you hear your servant cursing you. For many times, also, your own heart has known that even you have cursed others." What wisdom! If you embrace the truth in this Scripture, it will save you a great deal of pain. You can guard your heart against maliciousness by dismissing unkind comments before they penetrate.

More Determined Than The Devil

The enemy is relentless. I will never forget the day that the Lord said these words to me: "Jo, you need to be more determined that the devil." That was probably the first time I stopped to think about how much satan perseveres! He is crafty and he is always looking for the next plot to prevent you from serving Jesus. The good thing is that there is nothing new under the sun (see Ecclesiastes 1:9). The devil has no new tricks, but what he lacks in creativity, he makes up for in persistence. Make a decision today that you will be more determined than the devil! You have access to all the power and might of God to maintain your course.

Ephesians 6:10 (AMP) says, "In conclusion, be strong in the Lord [be empowered through your union with Him]; draw your strength from Him [that strength which His boundless might provides]." As you draw on His strength, you will be able to overpower the enemy. This is necessary because satan seeks ways to trap God's people. Jesus was surrounded by leaders who hated Him. They detested the freedom from the law that He preached, and they could not stand His popularity. The apparent success and fame that Jesus enjoyed made many envious.

Entrapment

Men who should have followed Jesus while He walked the earth wanted Him dead. Driven by jealousy, they tried to trap Him. Perhaps you have known the pain of being envied by your peers. It can cause terrible attacks. The leaders in Jerusalem asked Jesus loaded questions and scrutinized His every move. Luke 11:53-54 (AMP) says, "As He left there, the scribes and the Pharisees [followed Him closely, and they] began to be enraged with and set themselves violently against Him and to draw Him out and provoke Him to speak of many things, secretly watching and plotting and lying in wait for Him, to seize upon something He might say [that they might accuse Him]."

Men secretly watched Jesus, plotting His downfall. If your words and actions have been scrutinized by people you once trusted, it may have made you feel exposed and insecure. It can feel like a form of betrayal. If you have been judged and criticized, the attacks may have been debilitating. My husband and I have always agreed that we loved our church so much that we would be lifelong members, even if we weren't the senior leaders. During a season of accusation, I sat with our leadership team reflecting on the events that we had all endured. I broke down as I shared: "Right now, I don't feel safe in our church." Feeling like everyone is picking your every word apart can be soul destroying. If you have experienced that pain, God wants to heal your heart. As we close this chapter, I would like to lead you in prayer. Open your heart as you pray about the issues that have affected you.

Heavenly Father,

I come to You with my heart wide open. Things that have been said have hurt me. (*Now tell the Lord exactly what was said and how it made you feel, be as honest as you can.*) The words felt harsh and cruel, and I realize the damage that they have done. I can now see satan's strategy to use buried pain to bury my potential. So today I choose to demolish the devil's plans against me.

The slurs of others have made me dislike myself. Their criticism tarnished my view of me. It's horrible, Lord. Their attacks made me feel exposed and embarrassed. (*Now tell the Lord exactly how people's criticism made you feel about yourself.*) But I now realize that shame is a plan of the enemy to make me hide. Today, I make a decision that I will not cover up, instead I will allow You to heal my heart. I refuse to come under a cloud of shame. I surrender every corner of my soul and ask You to heal me deep inside. Please wipe away any sense of shame or uncleanness that may have remained.

Being judged made me doubt myself. Words spoken caused me to feel disqualified and condemned. (*Once again, tell your Heavenly Father about any judgement that has hurt you. Tell Him what happened and how it made you feel.*) I realize now that the plan of the enemy is to make me feel disqualified. Thank You Jesus that You made the way for me to enjoy complete freedom from guilt and condemnation. I will no longer tolerate any ideas that I am not qualified to continue serving You. Those are the lies of the enemy. I declare that I will arise stronger than ever and that I will fulfill my highest potential.

No weapon formed against me shall prosper. Every tongue that has risen against me shall be condemned. I will not allow pain, shame, self-doubt, and hatred to keep me out of my purpose. As I begin the next chapter, I am ready for a life changing healing encounter in Your presence. All fear and intimidation will be broken off me as my heart is healed.

Have Your way I pray,

In Jesus' name,

Amen.

Chapter 3

GOD'S PURPOSE

"It hurts, Lord," I cried out, "These attacks are tearing me apart!" I wasn't just weeping, I was howling from my belly. An isolated field in the countryside near our home became my secret place during that season. Any time hurt built up, I went there to meet with the Lord. I never ignored the way I felt. I did not bury my pain. I brought it to my Wonderful Counsellor. Day by day, week after week, He restored my soul. That particular storm lasted about four months. Poisoned arrows were shot at me and many people that I love also came under fire. The shock alone could have knocked me off my course if I had not known how to deal with the pain.

The devil relentlessly accuses Christians, he does not stop, day or night (see Revelation 12:10). It is therefore almost inevitable that you will be charged of terrible wrongdoing at some point during your life. Whether there is any truth or not in the allegations, coming under fire hurts. The more you do to build God's kingdom, the more likely it is that you will be attacked. But you do not need to be afraid of accusation, you just need to know how to deal with it, and how to be healed every time you are judged. If you keep your heart tender through every onslaught, the Lord will turn your situation around. Genesis 50:20 (NIV) says, "You intended to harm me, but God intended it for good to accomplish what is now being done, the saving of many lives." The key to your turnaround is the healing of your heart.

Your Heart's Design

Your heart was not designed to house pain. You were made in the image of God: "So God created man in His own image; in the image of God He created him; male and female He created them." (Genesis 1:27) If you were made to reflect your Heavenly Father, then your soul was also made in the image of His soul. He formed your heart for the same purpose as His: for the giving and receiving of love, for fellowship. God designs everything for its purpose. Fish were formed with underwater breathing apparatus (gills) to enable them to thrive in the water. The human heart was designed to be sensitive so that men and women could absorb the very atmosphere of God: love and glory. The delicate nature of your soul means that pain can cause a great deal of damage. Even if your heart has been hardened by the difficulties of life, harsh blows can be debilitating, the wounds just get buried below a toughened exterior.

Looking back at seasons when one accusation after another was leveled against me, I can honestly say that I am grateful for those experiences. We don't learn much on the mountaintop. The place of growth is in the valleys of our lives. Every time I have been attacked, I have been healed, and my heart has been enlarged. Not only that, but I have also gained wisdom that has prepared me for the next level. When you love the Lord and desire to fulfill His purpose, you can be certain that everything you go through will work together for your good. Romans 8:28 (NASB) is clear: "And we know that God causes all things to work together for good to those who love God, to those who are called according to His purpose." The devil will not have the last laugh. If you surrender to the Holy Spirit and seek Him for your healing, you will come out the other side stronger. Let's look at the vital steps.

1. If It Hurt, You Need To Be Healed

If you had been the victim of a terrible stabbing, you would seek immediate medical help. It is no less important that you ask the Lord to heal your heart when you have been wounded by words.

Words have the power to bring death and life (see Proverbs 18:21). That suggests that cruelty has the power to be fatal. I don't think negative comments can end your physical life. However, brutal insults can crush your soul. Some children who were told by teachers that they are useless have written themselves off as adults. Throwaway comments can mark a person's view of their own worth. They can cause people to give up on their dreams and settle for a life of mediocrity.

Sally was a passionate scientist even as a child. Her dream was to study hard to become a doctor. During her teenage years, an art teacher mocked Sally's work and declared, "You can't draw for the life of you!" Sally felt humiliated and became ashamed of her efforts. She returned to her seat feeling like a failure. But Sally's hurt feelings were only the first injury. Those negative words kept on speaking. Despite her flair for biology and desire to study medicine, Sally decided she would have to drop the subject. She reasoned that she could never succeed in biology because she would be unable to draw diagrams. Eight cutting words caused Sally to close the door to her dreams to be a doctor.

If you have been torn apart by criticism or judgement, it is vital that you ask the Lord to heal your heart. If certain words have stuck, they are the ones you need to deal with first. The Bible describes accusations as fiery darts. They can pierce even the thick skinned and get lodged in your soul. Because they entered as words, they need to leave the same way. Tell the Lord what was said and how much it hurt. Explain what wounded you the most and why. Remember, Jesus is your Wonderful Counsellor (see Isaiah 9:6). Counselling only works when a client shares their most intimate thoughts and feelings. Create some time alone with the Lord to pour out your heart in His presence. As you describe the distress you experienced, in as much detail as possible, buried pain will be dislodged. As you offload your burdens, He will restore your soul and fill you afresh with His love.

It's not just the major attacks that need to be healed. The Bible says that words shape our lives. We are made in the image of God who said, '"Let there be light"; and there was light' (Genesis 1:3). When we speak, our words carry power. When they are encouraging or inspiring, they bring life. However, when words are unkind, they can be crushing. Even a small splinter can cause problems if you don't dig it out. Words penetrate. They find a way into your heart. If you have been hurt by throwaway comments, you may find yourself rehearsing what was said. Just as little splinters must be unearthed to avoid infection, any hurtful comments that have stuck in your soul or dented your confidence must be removed.

Ask the Holy Spirit to reveal anything spoken over you that made you feel like you're not enough. Proverbs 20:27 (TPT) says, "The spirit that God breathed into man is like a living lamp, a shining light searching into the innermost chamber of our being." We have been conditioned by culture to ignore emotional pain, but King David understood the importance of opening up his soul to the Lord. He prayed with an open heart in Psalms 139:23 (TPT) "God, I invite your searching gaze into my heart. Examine me through and through; find out everything that may be hidden within me. Put me to the test and sift through all my anxious cares." Pause for a moment and ask the Holy Spirit to shine His light into the hidden places of your heart and reveal any words that have hurt you, any accusations that have affected your outlook. Make a note of anything that the Lord brings to your remembrance.

The same David who asked the Lord to search his heart, poured out his pain in God's presence. Even though David was a fierce warrior that fought many battles, he did not ignore the fact that verbal attacks hurt. He shared the pain of being slandered with the Lord in Psalms 64:3 (NLT): "They sharpen their tongues like swords and aim their bitter words like arrows." He brought hurtful words to the Lord in prayer and shared his struggles with God. In fact, the king brought his pain to God just as faithfully as he praised God. Because he offloaded his hurts in God's presence, his heart was free to worship. In the same way, your Heavenly Father wants you to be healed anywhere you hurt. I will lead you in a prayer of restoration at the end of this chapter.

2. Remember, You Are Righteous

Sometimes, the charges brought against you have an element of truth. They may even be entirely factual. The enemy wants you to be drowned in guilt and shame. As we revealed in chapter two, just because you messed up, that does not make accusation legitimate. Jesus paid the price for your mistakes on the cross. 1 John 1:9 is clear: "If we confess our sins, He is faithful and just to forgive us our sins and to cleanse us from all unrighteousness." The Holy Spirit convicts, satan accuses. Conviction seeks to bring repentance and forgiveness. Accusation aims to expose and condemn. It is time to silence satan's lies and experience the joy of knowing you are righteous in Christ.

You and I need to submit to the righteousness that comes from God. Most of the New Testament is written in Greek, while the Old Testament is written in Hebrew. The Greek for submit is hypotassō which means to subordinate, obey, be obedient, to submit yourself under. Righteousness in Christ is not just a perk of salvation, it is a statement of fact. Romans 10:3 says, "For they being ignorant of God's righteousness, and seeking to establish their own righteousness, have not submitted to the righteousness of God." To help understand the meaning of this verse, let's look at it in the Passion version: "And since they've ignored the righteousness God gives, wanting instead to be acceptable to God because of their own works, they've refused to submit to God's faith-righteousness." (Romans 10:3, TPT)

This is amazing news! Not only is your righteousness a gift, but God also expects you to remain righteous by faith. Your own works can never justify you, it is Christ's perfect work that justifies you. Jesus rejoices when you recognize deep down that you are spotless because of His forgiveness. Romans 10:4 says, "... Christ is the end of the law for righteousness to everyone who believes." Jesus alone makes you clean. Romans 10:10 (NIV) explains further, "For it is with your heart that you believe and are justified..." Jesus wipes away the mud that has been slung at you and makes you completely clean.

Of course, it is tempting to try to justify yourself. After all, things may have been said that question your character. But God's ways are higher than our ways. Jesus didn't defend Himself when He was accused of blasphemy. You don't need to prove yourself either. True freedom comes when you get a revelation deep down that the blood of Jesus wipes away every smear. When you believe that Jesus made the way, you will enjoy the peace of knowing that you are righteous in Christ. 2 Corinthians 5:21 says, "For He made Him who knew no sin to be sin for us, that we might become the righteousness of God in Him." It's time to shut the mouth of the enemy. It's time to lay down every weight of guilt. The price has been paid for you to enjoy the peace of righteousness in Christ.

3. A Gift In Disguise

Imagine a big diamond wrapped up in old brown paper, perched just out of reach on the branches of a bramble bush. It might be hard to reach, and the thorns might scratch, but it would be worth the struggle! Forgiving is the same way. It can be hard and may be a painful process, but forgiving is a precious treasure that releases untold blessings. Finding a gigantic diamond would open doors of opportunity and release you into financial freedom. In the same way, forgiveness is laden with benefits, but they last forever.

Accusation is destructive. It can wreck reputations and ruin relationships. The devil uses the pain and injustice to tempt you into holding unforgiveness. However, no matter what has been said or done, forgiveness paves the way for your freedom. When we hold something against someone, we inadvertently hold onto that person. Because we won't let go of what they did, we cannot let go of them either. Unforgiveness keeps us bound to the events and the people of the past. That means that you bring that person and those bitter experiences with you wherever you go. When upset or anger is buried inside, you stay connected to the people who caused you that pain. You bring them with you into every situation and every new relationship.

When unforgiveness is left to fester, it produces resentment and bitterness. Resentment can eat you up on the inside. It's that nagging feeling that you've been treated unfairly. Job 5:2 (NLT) says, "Resentment destroys the fool..." It is unwise to ignore resentment because it is destructive. It empowers old wounds to cause more pain. When you let go, you will experience glorious freedom. Bitterness is one of the most dangerous heart issues. It causes untold trouble and defiles those closest to us. Acts 8:23 says, "For I see that you are poisoned by bitterness..." When we do not forgive, we are in danger of infecting our hearts and choking the life out of our relationship with God. That is why satan works hard to make us hold onto our hurts. My book Destiny Blockers provides detailed steps to freedom from the foul disease that is bitterness. Unforgiveness is the devil's way of making the pain of the past even more potent. However hard it is to let go, it is more than worth the effort.

Another devastating side effect of unforgiveness is the quest for revenge. If we gloat when those who have wronged us fail, we are setting ourselves up as a judge and straying into God's domain. Romans 12:19 says, "Beloved, do not avenge yourselves, but rather give place to wrath; for it is written, "Vengeance is Mine, I will repay," says the Lord." Unforgiveness weighs heavy in our hearts. It causes negative emotions to fester. They infect our lives and relationships. They keep us bound and hardened. Proverbs 20:22 (NLT) says, "Don't say, "I will get even for this wrong." Wait for the Lord to handle the matter." To forgive, we need to let go of all our anger and every sense of injustice. We must give up our quest for revenge. God is the judge. Whether it's a co-worker, a brother, a leader, a spouse or parent who deeply wounded you, the relief when you fully forgive will be tremendous.

Anything Against Anyone

Mark 11:25-26 gets me every time: "And whenever you stand praying, if you have anything against anyone, forgive him, that your Father in heaven may also forgive you your trespasses. But if you do not forgive, neither will your Father in heaven forgive your trespasses." It says if you have *anything* against *anyone*, forgive. There is no grudge too small nor any offense too big. We cannot hold anything against anyone. God is asking you to lay down the heavy weight of unforgiveness. He is asking you to release those who hurt you from any debt you feel they owe.

Jesus wipes away all our wrongdoings even though we deserve to be punished. He forgave the men who sentenced Him to death while He hung on the cross in agony. He wants us to imitate Him. But remember how I started this section. Forgiveness is a gift in disguise. It will cut the cord that connects you with the people who caused you pain. It will set you free from the events of the past. It will silence the constant murmurs of resentment and wash away the defilement of bitterness. But it does not stop there. It will release healing, peace and freedom into your life. Forgiveness also forges a precious closeness with your Heavenly Father. I will lead you in prayer to release forgiveness at the end of this chapter.

When You Struggle To Let Go

When the attacks you've suffered led to catastrophic consequences, it can be hard to forgive. Maybe the maliciousness of others led to the breakdown of a precious relationship or perhaps it destroyed your ministry. Jesus showed us how to forgive when it is desperately difficult. Our God was spat at and mocked publicly by men He created. A blood thirsty crowd that He served and loved throughout His short life chanted, "Crucify Him!" Jesus was whipped until

His flesh was ripped off His back. Think about the pain that our Lord endured as He hung upon the cross. Struggling for every breath, Jesus was suffocated for our sins. I do not believe that it would have been easy for Him to forgive. Yes, Jesus is fully God, but He also walked the earth as a man.

Jesus gave Himself a reason to forgive. He said, "... they don't know what they're doing." (Luke 23:34). He chose to believe that they did not understand their actions. He did not amplify any evil intent. In fact, Jesus minimized their wrongdoing in His eyes. As a result, He was able to forgive. Following a painful season, even after praying prayers of forgiveness, I still had a hard heart towards someone who hurt me. In the end, I asked the Lord for His help, I asked Him to give me a reason to forgive. He opened my eyes to how misguided my accuser had become, this helped me to let go once and for all, and the relief was wonderful.

If your heart remains hard towards anyone, that is a sure sign that you have not yet fully forgiven. Matthew 18:35 makes it clear that true forgiveness is not just a choice or a prayer, it comes from the heart. If you still feel any animosity towards the one who has hurt you, ask the Lord for His help. Seek Him for a reason to let go of all anger. God knows the ones who have caused you pain, and He understands you completely.

4. Leave them to God

God is rich in mercy (see Ephesians 2:4). He wants you to be restored every time you stumble. In the same way, His desire is that those who have wounded you fulfill their purpose. If they are saved, then they are also God's children. He takes parenting seriously and desires that all His sons and daughters flourish irrespective of their failings. God's people are also His servants. Even as our Master, the Lord is committed to our success. Romans 14:4 (NLT) says, "Who are you to condemn someone else's servants? Their own master will judge whether they stand or fall. And with the Lord's help, they will stand and receive his approval."

The Holy Spirit does not need a deputy to help Him manage the affairs of men. He knows what is best for you, for me and for those who have hurt us. Our merciful God does not want to hear prayers motivated by the desire for vengeance. Romans 12:19b says, "Vengeance is Mine, I will repay," says the Lord." The Lord does not want us asking Him to punish those who hurt you or me. Even asking for justice is risky. We can't be selective about such a request. If you want justice (rather than mercy) against those who have wronged you, you must also expect justice (rather than mercy) in your own life.

Jesus is clear: "But I say to you, love your enemies, bless those who curse you, do good to those who hate you, and pray for those who spitefully use you and persecute you" (Matthew 5:44). We walk in love when we speak God's blessings over those who made our lives difficult. Hanging in agony on the cross, Jesus asked His Father to forgive those who sent Him to His death. You and I are called to follow in the footsteps of Jesus and love the way He loved. Lay down any desire for the demise of those who have wounded you. Instead, ask the Lord to fill you with His love.

I will never forget a day that I was complaining to the Lord about a lady that had made my life difficult. Assuming He would comfort me, I was taken aback when He retorted sternly, "Be quiet! She was whining to me about you earlier!" I realized how wearisome it must be for God to have His children whining about each other and calling it prayer. I apologized and became intolerant of any gripes about God's people.

Of course, it is important to pour out your heart to the Lord when you have been hurt. However, complaining to God (or your friends) about His people is a completely different matter. Love believes the best and keeps no record of wrongs (see 1 Corinthians 13:4-7). Even when we have been hurt, God's desire is that we walk in love towards the people who have wronged us (see Ephesians 5:2). That doesn't necessarily mean that you will maintain a relationship. It does mean that you will wish the best for them from your heart and pray for them when you think of them. To do that, your heart needs to be healed.

Eradicating Accusation From Our Own Lives

When someone hurls allegations at you, the temptation is to fight back. The problem is that accusation is always wrong, even if it is provoked. Remember that satan is the accuser of the brethren (see Revelation 12:10), so that job is taken. The enemy wants to suck you in to a mudslinging match. The Lord wants to lead you away from the fray. Resist the urge to react, and instead, place your case in God's capable hands. Take the high road, which is the low road of humility.

If you are particularly discerning, or if you have a heart to see injustice eradicated, then you may have a keen eye for wrongdoing. This is because God designs people for their purpose. In an attempt to block your destiny, satan will try to use your gifts to trap you. The enemy will try to stir judgement in your heart. He will tempt you to condemn people's actions and motives because he knows that if he can get you judging their hearts, he can make your journey difficult. Protecting your heart must be a priority for the sake of your destiny.

Remember, condemnation is the devil's counterfeit of conviction. If you speak to somebody with blame and judgement, they will feel attacked. So, when you judge, you lose, the people that you are addressing lose, only the devil wins. We need to protect ourselves from becoming accusers. The difference between seeing error and accusing is not the involvement of your tongue, it is the attitude of your heart. When I am accusing, my heart is hard, mercy is absent, I am full of judgement and blame. It's your heart that you need to watch.

5. The Gift Of Vindication

"I won't vindicate you too soon," the Lord spoke clearly. It was just weeks after a major character assassination had been leveled against me and I was still feeling raw. I harbored the Word of the Lord in my heart throughout that season. I could understand the wisdom in God holding back any public affirmation. Although seasons of shaking can be painful, sometimes they are necessary. Haggai 2:6-7a (NLT) says, "For this is what the Lord of Heaven's Armies says: In just a little while I will again shake the heavens and the earth, the oceans and the dry land. I will shake all the nations..."

Notice that God does the shaking. Of course, He is not the author of pain or confusion, but He shakes our hearts and lives for a purpose. Hebrews 12:27 (NLT) explains: "This means that all of creation will be shaken and removed, so that only unshakable things will remain." The Lord shakes to purify us, to cleanse the dross from our hearts. He shakes so that superficial relationships will be disconnected. Not everyone is called to journey with you long term. Your love for people may cause you to hold on to connections that were intended for a season, not for life.

Why Do I Want To Be Vindicated?

When the Lord told me that my vindication would not come too soon, I imagined that He wanted to wait until only those who were called to walk with us in the future remained. I longed for my name to be cleared but was happy to wait for God's timing. God healed my heart and restored my faith in people. Every trace of offense was replaced with compassion and love for those who had hurt me. The Lord broke the spirit of intimidation off my life and brought me into greater liberty. God gave me more wisdom, discernment and understanding about people's hearts and His ways. I could see the personal growth that the shaking had produced in me. Then one day, as I was talking to the Lord, I heard my heart whisper, "Lord, I don't need to be vindicated."

As those words left my heart, an invisible veil lifted from my eyes. "Oh my goodness!" I exclaimed, "My need for vindication was rooted in a concern for my reputation." I realized that I wanted people to know my heart. Jesus, in contrast, "... made Himself of no reputation..." (Philippians 2:7b). Sometimes vindication comes when we no longer need to be justified. Instead, vindication is for the gospel's sake, so that God's will can be done through His vessels.

Have things been said that muddied people's opinions of you or your integrity? When there are questions being asked about your character, it can hinder God's purposes coming to pass. While your priority needs to be the restoration of your soul, God is also concerned with your reputation. He takes the defense of His people seriously. Psalms 37:6 (NLT) offers a phenomenal promise: "He will make your innocence radiate like the dawn, and the justice of your cause will shine like the noonday sun." Listen to the same verse in the Message: "He'll validate your life in the clear light of day and stamp you with approval at high noon." (Psalms 37:6 MSG). That's God's heart towards you!

But remember, vindication is God's job. If you give the Lord your reputation, He will ensure it is restored at exactly the right time. Your reputation is useful when God uses it for His purposes. Like many things in God's kingdom, it's when we die to self that He is able to raise us back to life. The Lord promised to make Abraham's name great. In Christ, you have access to the promises God made to Abraham. Galatians 3:16 says, "Now to Abraham and his Seed were the promises made. He does not say, "And to seeds," as of many, but as of one, "And to your Seed," who is Christ." That means you can stand on God's promise to make your name great too. Great names open great doors for the gospel's sake. Great names attract kingdom favor. The Lord wants to turn your situation around for His glory.

6. Answering Your Accusers

Every time my husband and I have faced accusations, God has instructed us to walk through the storm by humbling ourselves. It is tempting to try to justify yourself or prove your innocence. It would be easy to get embroiled in pulling apart the details of their charges. But when someone is angry enough to make public accusations, they probably don't want to hear your defense. Their aim may well be to expose your weaknesses. As a result, nothing you say will be enough. You would probably find yourself in the middle of an ugly mudslinging match. Romans 8:33 says, "Who shall bring a charge against God's elect? It is God who justifies."

God was very clear about the way that we should respond to allegations made against us: go the low road. That meant humbling ourselves and apologizing for any hurt that we had caused. We have been pastoring for almost three decades. By God's grace, we have done a great deal of good in that time. By the same token, we have doubtless made many mistakes and unwittingly hurt precious people. Humbling yourself is tough on the flesh but good for the soul, and it keeps you on the right side of God. He hates judgement. He will not tolerate pride, but He draws near to those who humble themselves.

The sons of God are led by the Spirit of God, not by other people's comments or questions. When someone is charging you, sometimes no answer is the right answer. 1 Peter 2:23 (NLT) says, "He did not retaliate when he was insulted, nor threaten revenge when he suffered. He left his case in the hands of God, who always judges fairly." Refusing to engage with accusations can be liberating. As we saw earlier, it is all too easy to get embroiled in a catalog of issues. When you leave a situation in the hands of God, you demonstrate that you trust Him, and you give Him the power to work things together for your good.

Matthew 21:23b-27 tells the story of a time when Jesus was challenged by religious leaders: "By what authority are You doing these things? And who gave You this authority?" But Jesus answered and said to them, "I also will ask you one thing, which if you tell Me, I likewise will tell you by what authority I do these things: The baptism of John—where was it from? From heaven or from men?" And they reasoned among themselves, saying, "If we say, 'From heaven,' He will say to us, 'Why then did you not believe him?' But if we say, 'From men,' we fear the multitude, for all count John as a prophet." So they answered Jesus and said, "We do not know." And He said to them, "Neither will I tell you by what authority I do these things." Jesus was not intimidated by their insinuations or their demands. He felt no obligation to enter into their scheming or cross-questioning and He maintained control of the situation.

Of course, there will be times when it is right to answer charges made against you. Even then, please do not react, instead respond. When we react, we are on the back foot, and feel compelled by pressure and circumstances to give an immediate explanation. Proverbs 25:28 explains "Whoever has no rule over his own spirit is like a city broken down, without walls." Reacting makes us vulnerable to the enemy's agenda. In contrast, when we respond, we give ourselves time to consider the best course of action. It allows you to pause, choose what you are going to say, plan how you will say it, and when. Learning to respond in potentially stressful situations is a hugely valuable life skill. It will give you back control of your thoughts and your emotions in the midst of difficulties.

Stand Behind Your Savior

Jesus' disciples often came under fire. They were accused of rebellion and irreverence. Luke 5:30 says "the scribes and the Pharisees complained against His disciples, saying, "Why do You eat and drink with tax collectors and sinners?" They criticized the disciples' lifestyle choices. Just a chapter later, Luke 6:1b-2 tells another story, "... His disciples plucked the heads of grain and ate them, rubbing them in their hands. And some of the Pharisees said to them, "Why are you doing what is not lawful to do on the Sabbath?" Their every move was being watched and their actions were being judged. But the disciples *never* had to defend themselves! Jesus always answered their accusers.

Let's look at the two examples I just shared. In Luke 5:31, "Jesus answered and said to them, "Those who are well have no need of a physician, but those who are sick." The Lord did not ask His disciples to vindicate themselves, He took care of the accusations. In the same way, we see our Savior rebutting the judgements in Luke 6:3-4, "But Jesus answering them said, "Have you not even read this, what David did when he was hungry, he and those who were with him: how he went into the house of God, took and ate the showbread, and also gave some to those with him, which is not lawful for any but the priests to eat?" Jesus answered His disciples' critics then and He will do it today.

You can stand behind your Savior every time you are charged. As long as you ask Him to forgive you any time you mess up, Jesus will defend you. We can learn from the donkey that carried Jesus into Jerusalem. If it had risen up to take the praises, Jesus would have fallen off. The donkey kept going and allowed Jesus to receive all the praise. In the same way, when you are praised, stay low and give it all to Jesus. If you give Him the praise, you can also give Him all the criticism.

7. Having The Right Attitude

Accusation feels wrong, it is cruel and causes damage. As a result, the desire for justice to be done can be immense. Everyone makes mistakes, so there will never be an accuser who has not fallen short. It can therefore be tempting to focus on the shortcomings of our persecutors. But the problem is that judgement can be a magnet for demonic attack. One of the reasons that the enemy likes you to internalize your pain is that he can use it as a weapon against you. Buried wounds cause destructive emotions to fester.

When your heart is healed, you foster an inner atmosphere for love and freedom.

Remember that God is just. Galatians 6:7 is clear, "Do not be deceived, God is not mocked; for whatever a man sows, that he will also reap." Unless we repent, we will pay for the wrong that we have done, and the same is true for our persecutors. Again, Colossians 3:25 says, "But he who does wrong will be repaid for what he has done, and there is no partiality." But God – who knows the motives and intents of each one of our hearts – is judge. He does not need our help to ensure justice is done. He is righteous and He will punish sin. In truth, that's why you need to have mercy on those who have hurt you. We need to let go of every ounce of anger and leave people in His capable hands.

Jesus modeled loving those who hated Him. His last thoughts before He died were for the wellbeing of those who wanted Him dead. The way that He was treated never diluted the strength of His affections. That's the definition of unconditional love. Jesus asked God to forgive His murderers because He understood the terrible consequences of their actions. He loved those who were enjoying His public humiliation just as much as He loved Mary and John who witnessed the horrific event. 1 Peter 3:9 (ESV) "Do not repay evil for evil or reviling for reviling, but on the contrary, bless, for to this you were called, that you may obtain a blessing." You will experience extraordinary liberty when you wish the best for those who have made your life hell.

8. Receiving Heaven's Hidden Blessings

When our daughter died, excruciating pain exploded in my heart. I ached in the deepest parts of my soul. Grief poured into secret places that I didn't know existed. It was as though the pain was so great that it stretched the very fabric of my heart. In the weeks and months after our princess died, our loving Heavenly Father took me on a deep healing journey. The Lord reached into the recesses of my soul and pulled out trapped pain. He restored my heart, one piece at a time. Out the other side, I noticed that I had greater love for others and more compassion than ever before. What the devil meant for our destruction, the Lord used for our transformation. Pain enlarged my heart.

Paul's Perspective

For me, the passing of our daughter gave me a new level of determination to see God's Kingdom being built on earth. I remember saying at Naomi's funeral: "Please pray in the weeks ahead that this won't leave a devastating mark on our lives, and pray that God will restore the breach." The Lord answered those prayers and gave us a new zeal to see people healed, restored and brought back into a real relationship with their Savior, Jesus Christ. The process of healing unfolded over the months following, but as the pain dissolved, the zeal remained. After a while, it became evident that even though the devil had fired his best shot, it woefully failed. God turned us into a river of healing and divine encounters for many.

When Solomon asked God to give him wisdom and understanding so that he could rule well, the Bible tells us that the Lord increased the size of the king's heart. 1 Kings 4:29 says, "And God gave Solomon wisdom and exceedingly great understanding, and largeness of heart like the sand on the seashore." It goes without saying that the Lord has an enormous capacity to love, His heart is huge. For you to carry His kindness to the people around you, you need a generous soul. One of the side of effects of being healed of deep hurts is that your capacity to love grows. When I look back at how the death of our daughter stretched my soul, I am amazed. What the enemy meant for harm, the Lord turned for good and He can do the same for you.

When we surrender our pain and ask the Lord to restore, He has a way of turning even our greatest trials around. Romans 5:3-4 says, "... but we also glory in tribulations, knowing that tribulation produces perseverance; and perseverance, character;

and character, hope." When you invite the Holy Spirit into every situation, He does a deep work in your heart which brings maturity, but not only that, it creates the very substance that the enemy attempted to destroy: hope. When you have gone to hell and back, and come out the other side stronger, hope breaks out inside. If you're not there yet, please stick with it. A time will come when you can look back at seasons of terrible suffering and see the goodness of God.

During the most difficult season of accusation I have experienced, I made a habit of going for walks in the countryside. I never buried my pain or ran away from the shame. I walked and talked with the Lord, sharing my heartbreak with Him in prayer. I agonized over every mistake I had made. Any time my heart hardened, I forgave again, I blessed, and I released the whole mess into God's hands. When I realized I didn't want to rely on leaders again, I entrusted my heart afresh to God and chose to trust His people. In truth, I didn't know how I was going to get through that season. But God did not just bring me through, He brought me out gloriously. When I look back now, I am amazed at the faithfulness of God.

How Did Our Example Respond?

Even though Jesus never made a single mistake, He was accused of breaking Jewish law and of blasphemy. Think about it, Jesus was charged with wrongdoing by the people He came to save. Compelled by love, He lived to die for their sins and ours, yet His critics constantly questioned His motives. When He healed the sick and brought freedom to captives, He was accused of being a servant of satan. Matthew 9:32-34 says, "As they went out, behold, they brought to Him a man, mute and demon-possessed. And when the demon was cast out, the mute spoke. And the multitudes marveled, saying, "It was never seen like this in Israel!" But the Pharisees said, "He casts out demons by the ruler of the demons."

Jesus' response to this malice was to help more people. Immediately after being accused of working for the devil, the Bible says, "Then Jesus went about all the cities and villages, teaching in their synagogues, preaching the gospel of the kingdom, and healing every sickness and every disease among the people." (Matthew 9:35) Jesus knew His struggle was not against flesh and blood, so He doubled His efforts to push back the forces of darkness and bring light to the world. Because Jesus was perfectly secure, even cruel accusations from men with great authority did not shake Him. He knew who He was, so those accusations were like water off a duck's back. This will be true for you.

As you allow the Lord to heal you of childhood wounds and life's inevitable hurts, you will become secure. That kind of security has nothing to do with your achievements or positions. It comes from knowing your worth as a dearly loved child of the Most High God. When you understand your value, unkind attacks from the general public will not hurt. When you are secure, even malicious words from strangers won't cause pain. When I was publicly torn apart, even in the thick of the storm, I did not worry what people thought of me. I did not feel ashamed. I remember enjoying an inner security even while I was under fire. What hurt me was the fact that my accuser was someone I loved dearly. Even when you are secure, the comments and actions of people you cherish and trust will have an impact. That's the price of love.

Happiness and Favor

Jesus hides abundance in the most unexpected places. Luke 6:22-23 says, "Blessed are you when men hate you, and when they exclude you, and revile you, and cast out your name as evil, for the Son of Man's sake. Rejoice in that day and leap for joy! For indeed your reward is great in heaven, for in like manner their fathers did to the prophets." When your name is slurred, God promises to bless you in two different time zones! Firstly, in the here and now, and secondly, in eternity. Your promise for abundance during your life on earth comes from the opening word of this verse: "Blessed". Listen to how the Amplified Bible explains what it means to be blessed: "Blessed (happy—with life-joy and satisfaction in God's favor and salvation, apart from your outward condition—and to be envied) ...) (Luke 6:22 AMP). God has a great reward in store for you.

But it does not stop there. He also promises to recompense you in heaven. There will be certain eternal rewards for those who suffer malicious attacks. When God heals your heart, your memories will start to fade. You will forget what was said and how it made you feel. But God will not forget! He will heal you, bless you on earth, and He will reward you in heaven! How good is that?! Joseph forgot terrible pain. Genesis 41:51 says, "Joseph called the name of the firstborn Manasseh: "For God has made me forget all my toil and all my father's house."

Let's bring all these issues to the Lord in prayer so that we can become better human beings out the other side of accusation.

Heavenly Father,

Accusation is painful and it has hurt me, Lord. It's not just the big things that have caused damage, throwaway comments have sometimes felt like daggers in my heart. I don't want any hurtful words to remain buried inside. I want to be healed and free from any lasting damage. So Lord, I ask You to shine Your light into the depths of my heart and reveal any painful scars. Holy Spirit of Truth, I ask You to gently uncover anything that is hiding in my heart. I surrender to Your love. Thank You that You are my Wonderful Counsellor and my closest friend, so I will talk to You about any pain that You reveal.

(Sit quietly in God's presence and allow Him to bring wounds to the surface. Once you know what He wants you to deal with in prayer, continue...)

Lord, it hurt me badly when those words were spoken, and those things happened. *(Now share in as much detail as possible what was said, why it hurt so much, how it made you feel. Be sure to tell God the exact words that were spoken. They entered your soul with words and need to be released the same way. Talk to your Wonderful Counsellor about everything you went through.*) I surrender my hurts to You, I don't want to hold them anymore. Take my pain away Lord and heal my heart. I receive Your wonderful healing love into the depths of my heart. Thank You that the power of those words is now broken. It's not what people say that is important anymore, it's what You say that frames my life.

Lord, I choose to forgive the people who hurt me the most. You always forgive me when I do wrong, so I freely forgive them. I know that I must have hurt others without even knowing, so I won't hold anger against those who have hurt me.

I forgive _____ (*insert the name of the person who has wounded you. You may need to repeat this prayer if several people have hurt you*) today. I forgive them for saying cruel things that hurt me. I forgive them for the things they did that caused me pain. I forgive you _____, I let you go, you don't owe me anything anymore. And Lord, I ask You to help _____ and bless them.

Thank You Lord that I am free from the arrows of accusation. Thank You for making the way for me. Thank You for Your goodness, Your kindness, Your love. Fill me to overflowing with Your precious presence.

I give You all the glory and all the praise for the things You have done.

In Jesus' name I pray,

Amen.

Part Two
BETRAYAL

"For it is not an enemy who reproaches me; then I could bear it. Nor is it one who hates me who has exalted himself against me; then I could hide from him. But it was you, a man my equal, my companion and my acquaintance."
Psalms 55:12-13

Chapter 4

THE PAIN OF BETRAYAL

Sitting in a scattered circle with our senior leaders, a man who had been with us since we planted the church stood up. Towering over me while pointing his finger in my face, he threw a list of allegations at me. The one that hurt the most went something like this: "And you should NOT be on staff in this church. You only have a position because you're married to him," he spun around and pointed at my husband, then continued, "The church should never have hired you, it should have appointed him!" Now he was waving his hand at our beloved Associate Pastor who was our most loyal, loving leader.

After that meeting, the man in question got on the phone and called many of our church members. The following Sunday, one third of our congregation was missing. We were shocked. One of the most difficult consequences of this man's allegations was that they seemed to unleash an atmosphere of dishonor. People suddenly felt justified in saying anything they liked. Folk questioned our motives for ministry, our preaching, our decisions, and our leadership. Normal respect was thrown to the wind. Honor was gone in a flash. In a moment, we had become prey.

After things began to settle, Paul and I got away for a few days. One evening, my husband asked me: "How are you?" I will never forget my reply, "I feel like I've been marched onto the platform of our church and stripped of my dignity in front of the entire congregation." His response was both compassionate and clear: "Our people need their church mother to be healthy. I'm giving you three weeks to get healed."

Jesus carried our hurts on the cross. Isaiah 53:4 says, "Surely He has borne our griefs and carried our sorrows…" That means that you and I don't have to tolerate any lasting pain. I would even go so far as to say, we must never give hurt a long-term home in our hearts. I knew I needed to be restored, and quickly.

Taking my husband's words seriously, I booked an appointment with our Wonderful Counsellor (see Isaiah 9:6). I realized that I had fallen out of love with the church. The problem is that it's not possible to genuinely love a person's head whilst disliking their body. I had to get my heart fixed. Alone in the presence of the Lord, I told Him that I felt betrayed and exposed. I explained that I felt stripped of every shred of dignity I once had. I cried as I talked to the Lord. While I lingered in God's presence, He poured His wonderful healing love into my heart. When I left my prayer closet, my soul was at peace, and I was ready to love the Body of Christ again.

Why Does It Hurt So Much?

Trust is the glue that holds relationships together. It creates security and enables you to relax in the knowledge that you are safe. When you trust a teacher, you have confidence dropping your child to school. When you rely on a doctor, you assume that they have your best interests at heart. Having faith in church leaders enables you to open your heart when the Word is preached. Friendship is built on mutual respect and confidence. The foundation of every marriage is trust. When you trust someone, you don't worry about what they will or won't do.

You can relax in the knowledge that they are dependable. Trust creates confidence.

When you are betrayed, trust is shattered. It is often shocking, and it can even change your view of the world. When someone behaves in ways that you never thought possible, it can cause you to reevaluate your outlook on life itself. It can leave you reeling with disappointment and feeling utterly disillusioned. It can smear your view of family, it can change the way you feel about church. If one or two teachers mislead you, all too easily you end up mistrusting educators in general. If a church leader lets you down, you can become suspicious of ministers. When you are forsaken by someone you really believed, it is a violation.

...But It Is Inevitable

The uncomfortable truth is that we will all experience betrayal's pain at some point or other. Relationships involve people, and people are flawed. It's not just that we will be betrayed, we could betray those who trust us. We won't keep every promise we make. We won't live up to every expectation. We could easily let others down and they may hurt us too. In fact, Jesus told us to expect betrayal: "Now brother will betray brother... and a father his child; and children will rise up against parents..." (Mark 13:12). I don't know what you have gone through or who has broken their promises. I do know that you have probably experienced broken trust too many times in your lifetime. It may have affected the way you relate to people. The enemy wants us to become guarded and wary as a result of life's difficulties. God wants us to grow to be more like Him.

The Complexity Of The Human Soul

Have you ever been unaware that you had some sort of medical issue? Perhaps that has been the case for someone you love? Maybe it was the presentation of one or two symptoms that caused you or your loved one to get it checked out. Just as we don't always know what's going on in our bodies, we are often unaware of the true state of our souls. This is not surprising, the Bible says that the heart of man is deep and prone to all kinds of self-imposed treachery. Psalms 64:6b says, "Both the inward thought and the heart of man are deep." Your heart is also complex. Even God – who knows everything – has to search to find out what is hiding inside. Jeremiah 17:9-10 (AMP) explains, "The heart is deceitful above all things... Who can know it [perceive, understand, be acquainted with his own heart and mind]? I the Lord search..." According to this verse, you and I really do not know what is going on deep down in our hearts at the best of times!

We need the help of the Holy Spirit to uncover buried pain that is weighing us down and holding us back in life. Proverbs 20:27 (TPT) says, "The spirit God breathed into man is like a living lamp, a shining light searching into the innermost chamber of our being." Please don't assume that you know the condition of your heart. Betrayal can be very damaging. Even after we think we have moved on, we may find that the pain has had a lasting impact. As we have seen, betrayal can shatter trust. It can wreck our perspective of life and change our attitudes towards people. Relationships are the foundation of happiness and lasting success. Betrayal is therefore one of the devil's trusted weapons to devastate destinies and spoil the lives of God's precious people.

Signs That Satan Is Exploiting Betrayal

Just as physical diseases can be diagnosed by examining symptoms, there are telltale signs that point to unresolved betrayal. The symptoms of a stroke differ to the signs of liver disease, so the indicators of betrayal are different to the symptoms of other heart issues. I will share some of the most common signs that you are still affected by betrayal. The following list is not exhaustive but highlights many common consequences. Before you assess yourself, please allow me to lead you in prayer:

Heavenly Father,

I open up my heart to you today. I don't want anything buried inside that will hinder my life, so I ask You to search my soul. Shine Your light into the depths of my being and reveal any lasting damage. Open my eyes to see the impact that betrayal may have had so that I can journey to freedom.

In Jesus' name I pray,

Amen.

The Symptoms

Have a look through the list below. If you see two or three of these telltale signs in your life, that suggests that you are suffering from the consequences of betrayal, even if your experiences were long ago.

- **Guarded** – You keep a close eye on the way people behave and watch what they say. When someone does something you don't like, you make a mental note and keep yourself at a safe distance. Satan used Scripture in an attempt to trick Jesus during the temptations in the wilderness (see Matthew 4:1-11). The enemy will try to use the Bible against you too. Where Proverbs 4:23 (NLT) says, "Guard your heart above all else for it determines the course of your life." The word for guard in the Hebrew is nâṣar and in this context, the Lord is asking you to take care of your heart in the way you would tend to a garden. Please don't see this as an instruction to be wary. It is an invitation to keep your heart open before God and soft towards people.

- **Trust** – It may be everyone, or it could just be certain personalities, but you struggle to trust. You see leaning on people as a risk. You find it hard to place confidence in someone or to reveal the real you. While the Bible never asks us trust everyone, having trust issues will hold us back.

When we are reluctant to put confidence in others, we are usually relying entirely on our own assessments of people. Proverbs 28:26 explains: "He who trusts in his own heart is a fool..."

- **Secrecy** – You view your privacy as a premium. You feel safe when your personal life is lived behind closed doors. You prefer to keep many of the details of your relationships and experiences confidential. It makes you feel strong and secure. Let's look at Proverbs 18:1 (ESV): "Whoever isolates himself seeks his own desire; he breaks out against all sound judgment." Keeping yourself to yourself is not God's plan for your life.

- **Barriers** – Perhaps you learned to build walls around your heart in childhood, or it may be a more recent habit. You've been hurt, so allowing people close seems like an unnecessary risk. You probably feel lonely at times because you don't allow many people to come close, but for you, that's a price worth paying. You relate to folk across the other side of an invisible wall. Although you suspect that others enjoy relationships more than you ever could, your walls make you feel strangely safe.

- **Wariness** – Caution comes naturally to you. You hesitate before opening up to people and find yourself being suspicious about the motives of others. When you see a 'red flag', you withdraw emotionally. You see wariness as a helpful means of avoiding hurt. Unfortunately, wariness is fueled by fear whereas wisdom flows from the knowledge of God. When you're healed of every trace of betrayal, you will be able to enjoy a life of love, where "believing the best" (see I Corinthians 13:7) becomes normal again.

- **Separation** – Even surrounded by family or friends, you often feel lonely. You watch others enjoy fellowship and affection but hold back. It feels as though there is an emotional gulf between you and the people you love. You can appear sociable and friendly, but deep down, you feel isolated.

- **Boundaries** – You work hard to create effective boundaries and you are all too aware when they are transgressed. When people don't respect your need for distance and respect, it makes you feel downtrodden, or even defiled. An overemphasis on boundaries is usually a sign of unhealed wounds.

- **Low or No Expectations** – It seems safer to "do it yourself" than to ask and be disappointed. When people make promises, you listen with skepticism. You don't often rely on others. It's the enemy who wants you to be fiercely independent so that you have to cope alone. God wants to heal your heart. Ecclesiastes 4:9-10 (NLT) says, "Two people are better off than one, for they can help each other succeed. If one person falls, the other can reach out and help. But someone who falls alone is in real trouble."

- **Superficial Connections** – Friendly you may be, but you keep relationships light and easy. If someone tries to dig too deep, you discretely close the door on that conversation and move onto something less personal. The less you have vested, the less you have to lose. God wants you to enjoy meaningful relationships.

- **Self-Sabotage** – When you examine the real reasons why your relationships fail, you can see a pattern of self-sabotage. You bolt before the other person has the chance to share their feelings. You reject others before they get the chance to reject you.

- **Independence** – You are an emotional loner. Even when you're surrounded by people, you keep yourself at a healthy distance from others. Some may call you aloof, you just say that you prefer your own company. You may like this about yourself, but please remember that right at the start, God said in

> Genesis 2:18b: "It is not good that man should be alone; I will make him a helper comparable to him."

If you recognize yourself in some of these descriptions, your Heavenly Father wants to restore your soul. Your inner wellbeing affects everything you do. That's why Proverbs 4:23 (TPT) says, "So above all, guard the affections of your heart, for they affect all that you are. Pay attention to the welfare of your innermost being, for from there flows the wellspring of life." This verse says, "Pay attention to the welfare of your innermost being…" Your heart matters, and it impacts your entire life. Your Heavenly Father wants to do a work inside that will bring joy and liberty. Before we go any further, let's pray:

Heavenly Father,

I open my heart to You. I don't want buried pain to shape my behavior anymore. I acknowledge that I have some symptoms of unresolved betrayal (*now tell the Lord which symptoms you see in yourself.*) I ask You to reveal every hidden hurt and lead me to genuine healing and freedom. Shine Your light into the depths of my soul and reveal old wounds that are still affecting my life. I entrust my heart to You.

In Jesus' name,

Amen.

Chapter 5

SATAN'S PLAN

Our adversary, the devil, has a foul plan for betrayal. He seeks to use your pain to block your purpose. The Hebrew for betrayal exposes his strategy: râmâ means to throw down, to shoot, to cause to fall. The reason we need to ask the Holy Spirit to reveal every hidden hurt is to ensure we close the door to satan's attempts to derail our destiny. Ephesians 4:27 (AMP) says, "Leave no [such] room or foothold for the devil [give no opportunity to him]." We need to ask the Lord to uncover known hurts, but also any hidden wounds that are secretly influencing our decisions. When the Lord heals our hearts, the enemy loses ground, and we are able to run our race with perseverance.

Over the next few pages, we will look at some of the different forms of disloyalty. As you read, if you identify with any of the pain we describe, don't wait until the end of this chapter to share your heart with the Lord. Instead, if you see yourself in the paragraphs that follow, pause for a moment. Tell your Heavenly Father what you went through, explain why it hurt so much. "...Pour out your heart like water before the face of the Lord..." (Lamentations 2:19 b). If you do this, you will begin to receive healing while you read. Our Master Restorer is by your side.

What Hurt The Most?

Betrayal comes in different shapes and sizes. The strange thing is that the depth of the pain does not always correlate with the ferocity of the blow. Sometimes small let downs by those you trusted implicitly hurt the most. In order to be healed, we need to face our pain. We can't leave it buried deep down. Romans 9:26 says, "And it shall come to pass in the place where it was said to them, 'You are not My people,' There they shall be called sons of the living God." When we allow the Holy Spirit to take us back to the place where things were said and done that hurt, we can begin our healing journey. When we share that pain with the Lord in prayer, we can be restored. Let's look at some examples of ways that you may have been disappointed by people. This isn't an exhaustive list so please keep your heart open as you read and ask the Lord to reveal any buried wounds. Let's pray as we begin to look at some of the most difficult forms of betrayal.

Heavenly Father,

I open my heart to you today. I don't know what's hidden within, but you know my heart, Lord. Search me, sift through all my anxious thoughts, shine Your light deep inside and reveal any buried pain. As You uncover any forgotten memories or hurtful experiences, heal my heart I pray.

In Jesus' name,

Amen.

Abandoned

You were designed by the Lord to enjoy unending love and fellowship. So when someone close forsakes you, the rejection can be soul destroying. If you have experienced this kind of pain, the Lord wants to heal your heart. Abandonment can happen at any stage in life. In childhood, at school, by family or friends, or by someone who promised to love you forever. If you have been deserted by someone you trusted, it probably caused deep pain.

Sometimes the greatest wounds are inflicted during childhood. Perhaps your mother left you or your father walked out on the family. We don't know what went on when David was growing up. However, something happened that made David feel forsaken by his parents. In Psalm 51:5, David says that he was conceived in his mother's womb in sin. Although it may well be a reference to original sin, I believe it is also much more straightforward than that. Perhaps Jesse, David's dad, had an affair and the shepherd boy was the result of a shameful mistake. Remember, when the prophet Samuel asked Jesse to present his sons, he somehow forgot David. Whether that disdain was based on the circumstances of his birth or just a personality clash, we don't know. However, we can be sure that the youngster didn't have a hugely happy home life. He felt forgotten.

Betrayal by mother or father is one of the most hurtful experiences that anyone can endure. When God created us, his plan was for every baby to be raised in an atmosphere of unconditional love. His intention was that you would grow up surrounded by the affection of both your mom and dad. Perhaps for you, like David, betrayal began at the beginning. Maybe your mom messed up or your dad fell short. When our parents consciously (or unconsciously) break our trust, it can distort our understanding of the world. I don't believe we can become our best until we have been restored and enjoy the fruits of inner security and peace. If that's not yet you, God wants to do a wonderful work within as you read.

King David expressed his pain in Psalms 27:10 (AMP): "Although my father and my mother have forsaken me, yet the Lord will take me up [adopt me as His child]." Sometimes because your life is the only one you have known, you wrongly assume that your suffering was acceptable. That's not the case. God wants to heal your heart.

Let me repeat some sentiments from the last chapter. Trust is the glue that holds relationships together. It builds a sense of safety and security. When trust is broken, it can be devastating. It can leave us reeling with disappointment and feeling utterly disillusioned. It can rock our view of people. If you have been abandoned by anyone you loved, you may be wary of drawing close to anyone. The Lord is able and willing to restore your shattered soul.

The Agony Of Abuse

When one person uses another person to satisfy their own sordid pleasures, the impact can be devastating. If someone uses their strength to overpower one who is physically weaker, it can be crushing. Each one of us was created in the image of God (see Genesis 1:27). You reflect your Creator who is majestic. The Lord intended for you to be treated with dignity and kindness throughout your life. If you have been abused, it is a violation that may well have shattered your self-worth. Sexual abuse can leave a man or woman feeling dirty and desecrated. Domestic violence can crush a person's sense of their own value. Verbal abuse can tear even a strong soul to pieces. When you have suffered in these ways, the enemy tries to mark you with shame. If this is you, my book, The Many Faces Of Shame, will bring you to healing and freedom.

King David's daughter Tamar was raped by her own brother when she was bringing him some food. 2 Samuel 13:11 (NLT) records what happened: "But as she was feeding him, he grabbed her and demanded, "Come to bed with me, my darling sister." Of course, she begged him to leave her alone, but 2 Samuel 13:14 says, "But Amnon wouldn't listen to her, and since he was stronger than she was, he raped her." Tamar's brother stole her purity, her dignity, and her hope. She left his presence crying bitterly. Sadly, she did not know how to be healed of the devastation and pain. As a result, she "remained desolate in her brother Absalom's house." (2 Samuel 13:20b)

Thank God that you and I can be fully restored after abuse. Psalms 147:3 (TPT) promises: "He heals the wounds of every shattered heart." If while you're reading, you are remembering something very painful, please don't run from this book, instead move it to one side, and start to tell Jesus, your Wonderful Counsellor, about the heartache you have suffered. Share how afraid you felt, tell Him about the physical and emotional pain you endured. Talk to the Lord. As you pour out your heart in His presence, you will feel the pain start to drain away. He will then fill your precious heart with His wonderful love.

Dishonesty

Psalms 51:6a explains something about God: "Behold, You desire truth in the inward parts..." In fact, it's not just that the Lord loves truth, He is The Truth (see John 14:6). Because you are made in the image of God, it is not surprising that you will want absolute honesty from those that you love. If people you trust turn out to be dishonest, the sense of betrayal can be colossal. Perhaps you have been cheated out of something that was rightfully yours. Maybe a family member or friend lied, causing you harm. I've heard too many stories of precious people being robbed of their inheritance by siblings, or even by their own parents.

One of the Bible's heroes experienced the same pain. His alleged crime? He was the fruit of his father's infidelity. Judges 11:1-2 (NLT) tells the story: "Jephthah of Gilead was a great warrior. He was the son of Gilead but his mother was a prostitute. Gilead's wife also had sons, and when these half-brothers grew up, they chased Jephthah off the land. "You will not get any of our father's inheritance," they said, "for you are the son of a prostitute." Jephthah was valiant according to God, but his brothers cut him out of his father's will. If you have been cheated by family or friends, it could have broken your trust. Please allow the Lord to restore your soul. Let's look again at Proverbs 4:23a (TPT): "So above all, guard the affections of your heart, for they affect all that you are. Pay attention to the welfare of your innermost being, for from there flows the wellspring of life." In short, when your heart is on the mend, every area of your life will benefit.

The Difficulty Of Disloyalty

A dear friend made a pertinent remark to me during a turbulent season in my life: "Loyalty is for difficulty." The moment she said this, the truth of her comment resounded around my heart. We can all be loyal when things are going well, but our steadfastness is tested during times of shaking. Speaking of shaking, Hebrews 12:27b says, "… the things which cannot be shaken may remain." We discover the extent of our loyalty, and the extent of the loyalty of our loved ones during difficulties. We all want our nearest and dearest to believe the best (see I Corinthians 13:7) when our character or motives are called into question. It's in the valleys of our lives that disloyalty hurts the most.

Sometimes disloyalty hits you like a bolt out of the blue. Perhaps you trusted someone and believed they would journey with you through every season, then without warning, they were gone. The grief of a relationship lost is bad enough, but the sense of letdown can make it feel unbearable. Then there are the occasions when people's hearts grow hard and cold over time. 2 Samuel 15:6 explains how Absalom's betrayal of his father King David was planned over the course of a few years: "In this manner Absalom acted toward all Israel who came to the king for judgment. So Absalom stole the hearts of the men of Israel." David had to face the painful truth that his son's disloyalty was rooted in a disdain towards his dad that he had been harboring for years.

In reality, it's very rare for someone to go from loving to disloyal in a moment. The hardening of a person's heart is almost always gradual. Small offenses may get dismissed, but not resolved. They may say, "It's not a problem" and brush it to one side. Offenses must not get buried in our hearts, they must be forgiven. That's why Mark 11:25 says, "And whenever you stand praying, if you have anything against anyone, forgive him, that your Father in heaven may also forgive you your trespasses." Whenever you get into God's presence, you need to forgive anything that you have against anyone. Forgiveness does not deny the impact of their actions, it chooses to let go of the debt that the offender owes. It chooses to give the matter to God and leave it with Him, forever. Small offenses on their own might not be a big deal. However, when one upset lands upon another, they can cause resentment to build.

Exposed

It is God's desire that your family and friends cover your nakedness when you make mistakes. Proverbs 17:9 (TPT) says, "Love overlooks the mistakes of others, but dwelling on the failures of others devastates friendships." Maybe you were deserted by people you trusted during a painful episode. Perhaps someone you knew for years walked away when you made a mistake. You may still beat yourself up for your failings. But Proverbs 24:16a (AMP) says, "... a righteous man falls seven times and rises again..." Even the righteous fall. What makes them different is that they get back up again.

"You must let it go," were the words that set me free. For many months, I had struggled to forgive myself for making a mistake that hurt some people I loved. I kept going over what I had said, wishing that I had handled things differently. Although I knew God had wiped away my wrong, I still felt responsible for the impact on others. When my brother, who is also a mighty prophet, spoke those words, the chains of regret broke. When you fall, you need a helping hand to get back up, not a slap in the face. If you are beating yourself up for a mistake you made or an opportunity missed, please don't listen to the devil's lies any longer. In the words of my brother, you must let it go.

The same devil that lures you into sin torments you with guilt when you fall. But when God forgives, he does not just cover over your mistakes, He washes them away. After that, your Heavenly Father miraculously forgets that you slipped in the first place. Hebrews 8:12b says, "...their sins and their lawless deeds I will remember no more." People blaming you for their misery does not mean that you are responsible. Each of us will give an account for our own heart and life. We will not have to answer for the behavior of others. Romans 14:12 is clear, "So then each of us shall give account of himself to God."

Genesis 9 tells the story of one of the Bible's first betrayals. "And Noah began to cultivate the ground, and he planted a vineyard. And he drank of the wine and became drunk, and he was uncovered and lay naked in his tent. And Ham, the father of Canaan, glanced at and saw the nakedness of his father and told his two brothers outside… 24 When Noah awoke from his wine, and knew the thing which his youngest son had done to him, He exclaimed, Cursed be Canaan! He shall be the servant of servants to his brethren!" (Genesis 9:20-22, 24-25 AMP)

Noah was Ham's father, his job was to love, protect and set an example. This passage tells the story of one of Noah's worst nights: he drank so much that he passed out in his room, naked. Noah behaved very badly, yet the Bible suggests that Ham's response to his father's drunkenness was the greater sin. Ham looked at his dad's nakedness and then talked to his brothers about their father's sorry state. I think he hoped his siblings would sneer. Everyone fails at one time or another. I am sure like me, you want friends and family to have your back when you trip up. That is what we all expect. Noah felt betrayed because his son exposed him when he needed to be protected.

You probably hope loved ones will remain loyal during the inevitable valleys of your life. I hope so too. But maybe someone you thought knew your heart doubted your motives. Perhaps a friend criticized you publicly or walked away when you needed them the most. The Noah breed of betrayal is particularly painful because you may hold yourself responsible. But 1 Peter 4:8b says, "… love will cover a multitude of sins." It is God's desire that you are protected when you are vulnerable. If you were deserted during a difficult season, the Lord wants to heal your heart.

Let Down By Leaders

Perhaps you have been let down by a minister, or maybe you have been betrayed by those you raised in ministry. Whether it is those leading you, or ministry helpers that you poured your life into, the pain of betrayal in church can be devastating. What we must make clear is that there is nothing that pleases the enemy more than you being hurt in God's house. Our adversary, the devil, wants you to back off from church and from building meaningful ministry relationships.

After years of feeling unwanted by his family, David must have been thrilled to find a new father figure. King Saul embraced David as a son and welcomed him into his home. Our young hero was loyal to the nation's leader and served him for several years as a musician and a warrior. When Saul suddenly turned against his spiritual son and accused him of treason, it must have broken David's heart. He was just 20 years of age and yet another father forsook him.

If you have been let down by a spiritual leader, it will probably have been very painful. We associate ministers with God, so when they fail us, we can feel that God has failed us. We attach extra importance to their words and their behavior. As a result, when we are betrayed by those in spiritual authority, it can be devastating. Remember, the enemy always wants to use your pain to block your purpose. Keeping away from church is one sure way of making a difficult time even harder. Please know that if you have been wounded by someone in authority, the Lord wants to heal your heart.

Paul's Perspective

There is often a desire in men to rise up and take vengeance on 'the traitor'. This could mean seeking an immediate opportunity to lash back. It might mean making a mental note and burying resentment, or it may be a case of waiting for the chance to pounce and get our own back. Many times our hearts become cluttered, and we end up activating all kinds of spiritual laws which work against us. For example, Mark 11:25 is painfully obvious in its assertion that our faith gets deactivated if we harbor such ideas. "Whenever you stand praying, forgive, if you have anything against anyone, so that your Father who is in heaven will also forgive you your transgressions." (Mark 11:25 NASB) Even in marriage (and Song of Songs 2:15 says it's the little issues that cause problems), the Bible is clear that the state of our hearts towards our spouse can accelerate or hinder our prayers (see 1 Peter 3:7-9).

Retaliation just isn't God's way. The desire for revenge can be overwhelming, but there are always two ways to do things: God's way or the hard way. In the early days of my ministry, I attended a leaders' prayer meeting in London, England. A man stood up in front of the whole group and said: "Paul the Lord has shown me that your heart is full of pride, and you need to repent!" I was dumbstruck. This wasn't a discipleship relationship, just a meeting of fellow leaders. His statement cut me like a sword. Every word resonated around my soul for days after. I was devastated. "Lord, what shall I do?" I cried out in desperation. Back came the reply, "What would Love do?"

The day of the next meeting, I went to a supermarket and loaded up my car with groceries for the man who wounded me. I didn't make a big song and dance, I just told him that I wanted to be a blessing. Nothing more was said. I relocated, so lost contact with this man. A year later, I ended up at the same dinner party as this gentleman. Towards the end of our meal, he stood up and said, "I would like to salute a dear brother. Everything I have learned about love, I've learned from this man, Paul Naughton." I was dumbfounded, but this time, in the most wonderful way. Sitting in the corner of the room that day a young lady looked on. "I'd like to get to know him," she thought to herself. Her name was Jo. She became Jo Naughton! What if I had not gone love's way? I could have missed out on so much.

Learning From Others

Our Church facility in London is surrounded by businesses owned by people from a particular ethnic group. Many of these folk are great businessmen, but I noticed something interesting about how they react to betrayal. One after another, these men would tell me how they had been ripped off or conned by one of the neighboring enterprises. It was as though they saw cheating each other as a sport! However, when the dust settled, they did not resent the people who cheated them, instead, they saw it as an occupational hazard.

I learned so much about forgiveness from these men. In fact, there is so much we can glean by looking at forgiveness in different cultures. Some ethnic groups are good at forgiving marital infidelity, whereas others would be crippled for life without divine intervention. During the early days of my salvation, I lived in Ireland where I worked for a community center which served the traveler community. I witnessed many vicious fights. If anyone from outside of their community tried to intervene, both parties would turn on them and beat them up instead. A week later, the men who had been violently fighting would be back on great terms with each other, as though nothing had happened! Such a conflict may take you or me years to forgive.

Jesus taught us to fully forgive every betrayal, and His way is the best way. Talking to his brothers years after they tried to destroy his life, Joseph said: "Am I in the place of God?" (see Genesis 50:19). He was explaining to these men that he had no right to hold their offenses against them. Joseph wanted them to know that he had let go of every ounce of anger. Joseph was saying that only God has the right to judge someone.

The Words Of Those In Authority

When God gives a person responsibility, He also gives them authority. This enables them to lead with power. However, when the words of someone in authority are full of negativity, this can be very harmful. We have all been hurt by unkind comments in school, among friends, and at work. But when the person being cruel has power in our lives, their words can be especially destructive. Proverbs 15:4 says, "A wholesome tongue is a tree of life, but perverseness in it breaks the spirit." When people have authority in your life, they have a responsibility to use their position to build. Perverse means crooked, twisted. When a teacher, parent or minister uses their authority inappropriately, it is perverse. It is a crooked use of power.

Cruel or critical words from those in authority can be so damaging that they can break your spirit. Let's look again at Proverbs 15:4 (NIV): "The soothing tongue is a tree of life, but a perverse tongue crushes the spirit." Wounding words from people in authority can crush your confidence. If you have been torn down by someone who was supposed to lift you up, the Lord wants to restore your soul and rebuild your self-belief.

Deserted By Destiny Helpers

It cost Moses everything to lead the children of Israel out of Egypt. He put his life on the line, not only when he challenged Pharaoh, but with every step he took into the wilderness. He had the faith to conquer Canaan, but the team he picked was full of fear. As a result, the assignment God gave him went from a month to a lifetime. You would think that the people would have been grateful to their selfless leader. On the contrary, Moses was constantly criticized by the masses and repeatedly betrayed by his leaders, even those that should have known his heart.

Numbers 16:1-3 (NLT) describes one such incident: "One day Korah... conspired with Dathan and Abiram... They incited a rebellion against Moses, along with 250 other leaders of the community, all prominent members of the assembly. They united against Moses and Aaron and said, "You have gone too far! The whole community of Israel has been set apart by the Lord, and he is with all of us. What right do you have to act as though you are greater than the rest of the Lord's people?"

Three men became offended at the role God gave to Moses and caused a group of influential leaders to turn on Moses. They accused their leader of pride and self-promotion. Moses probably invested in these men and could easily have been the one who first believed in them. Perhaps he trained them and nurtured their gifts. When you have poured yourself into people, it can be very painful if they walk away. Those who promised, "I will always have your back" may have led a charge against you. Because you allowed them into your life, they may know your weaknesses or vulnerabilities. Perhaps they used their access against you. If that's your experience, it is vital that you ask the Lord to heal every trace of pain. Unresolved trauma will influence our decisions and behavior if we don't seek the Lord for His healing.

Korah, Dathan and Abiram made awful accusations against Moses that must have hurt. However, nothing could have been further than the truth. The Lord Himself said Moses was humble, and yet the words of these offended leaders turned a whole community of people against God's servant. As we saw earlier in this book, accusation is from the enemy, and it is a foul weapon against God's people. One way it can damage its victims is by causing self-doubt. Maybe things have been said that have made you doubt your authority. Perhaps you have wondered if you even qualify for ministry. Remember, they did it to Moses, they did it to Jesus, so you're in very good company. Don't listen to the devil's lies. Ask the Lord to heal your heart, then get back up and lead again.

It Happened To Paul

Paul the apostle was deserted by many of his fellow laborers. Each time someone walked away from the apostle, he clearly felt hurt. They may have been leaving for legitimate reasons, but Paul felt abandoned. In 2 Timothy 4:10, he wrote, "Demas has forsaken me, having loved this present world, and has departed for Thessalonica—Crescens for Galatia, Titus for Dalmatia." Left almost entirely alone on the mission field, the apostle asked Timothy to join him quickly. Maybe you feel like leaders keep leaving your side. They may have all sorts of reasons, but to you it's a pattern and it makes you feel unappreciated and unsupported. If that's you, the Lord wants to heal your heart.

People leaving does not make you a bad leader, it makes you a leader. In 2 Timothy 4:16-17, Paul once again wrote about being deserted by his co-workers: "At my first defense no one stood with me, but all forsook me. May it not be charged against them. But The Lord stood with me and strengthened me..." Although watching people leave may be painful, it's important to remember that when you are weak, then the Lord will stand by you and make you strong (see 2 Corinthians 12:10).

Jesus understands how much maliciousness can hurt. Hebrews 12:3 says, "Consider Him who endured such hostility from sinners against Himself, lest you become weary and discouraged in your souls." He knows how much it can weigh you down and even break your spirit, but He urges you to lift up your eyes from your situation and to look into His face of love and acceptance. He endured the hostility of the cross so that you could be healed.

Leaders Lead People

Soon after King David's son Absalom tried to steal the crown from his father, David was betrayed again. A man called Sheba blew a horn and announced his desertion from the king. But he did not stop there. He proceeded to urge the people to flee from their leader and far too many listened. 2 Samuel 20:1-2 (NLT) tells the story: "There happened to be a troublemaker there named Sheba... Sheba blew a ram's horn and began to chant: "Down with the dynasty of David! We have no interest in the son of Jesse. Come on, you men of Israel, back to your homes!" So all the men of Israel deserted David and followed Sheba, son of Bicri.

Only the men of Judah stayed with their king and escorted him from the Jordan River to Jerusalem."

About 90% of the nation of Israel deserted King David on the word of one offended rebel. In today's society, a leader would probably use social media instead of a musical instrument to share their views. Perhaps leaders have publicly criticized your ministry. Maybe it is what they did not say that hurt, rather than what they did say. Either way, if you have been battered by backbiting or rumors, God wants to restore your soul.

Unfaithfulness and Broken Covenant

When two people promise to love each other forever, it creates a matchless sense of security. The covenant between a husband and wife is intended to be unbreakable. Speaking of marriage, Genesis 2:24 (ESV) says, "Therefore a man shall leave his father and his mother and hold fast to his wife, and they shall become one flesh." Covenant was never intended to be broken. The Hebrew word translated 'hold fast' is dâḇaq. It means to cling or join. As a result of this union, two become one flesh.

Because a husband and wife become one, the pain of a union breaking is immense. If you were to tear some of my flesh from my body, the ripping away would be agony. I think that goes some way to describing the pain of broken covenant between two who became one. If you have experienced the pain of unfaithfulness or abandonment, the Lord wants to heal you in the depths of your being. Such betrayal can shake you to the core. If you didn't see it coming, the shock can be almost unbearable. It can leave you wondering what's real. Unfaithfulness may have stripped you of your sense of dignity and made you feel like secondhand goods. If that's you, the Lord wants to heal your precious heart.

Speaking of adultery, Proverbs 5:8-9 says, "Remove your way far from her, and do not go near the door of her house, lest you give your honor to others..." Faithfulness honors, it makes a person feel treasured and protected. Infidelity strips its victim of their dignity. It can make a person doubt their value, it can crush confidence. Often, both parties end up feeling defiled. If you have suffered such pain, you may feel like you are a shadow of your former self. You probably feel humiliated and wonder how you can find your way back. I want you to know that God is able to restore your heart and wipe away any shame. One of Scripture's leading ladies understood the pain of sharing her husband with another woman. Genesis 29:31 (AMP) says, "...the Lord saw that Leah was despised..." The woman who would mother Judah suffered the pain of being hated by her own husband.

You may be reading knowing that you were the one who was unfaithful, or maybe you left your spouse. The same God who heals a shattered heart is able to restore your life. The enemy tries to smear you with guilt and shame after God has forgiven. Please don't listen to the devil's lies. Jesus hung on the cross to make you new. The only sin that is a problem with God is unconfessed sin. 1 John 1:9 is clear, "If we confess our sins, He is faithful and just to forgive us our sins and to cleanse us from all unrighteousness." After you have repented, you are washed clean and made righteous by the Lord.

You may have witnessed betrayal in your parents' marriage. The shock of such a situation can be devastating, especially when you see something that should never have happened. It can shake your world, break your trust and leave you bewildered. You could have watched your parents go through divorce while you were a child, or you may have seen their relationship break down later in life. The fact that 55% of American marriages end in divorce does not alleviate the pain. Everyone will suffer the loss of a loved one at some time in their life, but the fact that bereavement is common does not stop it hurting. If your family went through the heartbreak of separation, ask the Lord to shine His light into the depths of your heart and reveal any pain trapped inside. When hurts are hidden, they remain in the shadows of your soul. When they are revealed by the Holy Spirit, they can be healed.

Samson's wife betrayed her husband for money, her actions led to his downfall and ultimate death. Judges 16:18 tells the account: "When Delilah saw that he had told her all his heart, she sent and called for the lords of the Philistines, saying, "Come up once more, for he has told me all his heart." So the lords of the Philistines came up to her and brought the money in their hand." When a covenant relationship is broken, the pain can be almost unbearable. When someone you love is unfaithful, it can make you think that you're not enough, it can erode your sense of your own worth. If you have experienced such a backstabbing, the Lord wants to reach into the place of pain deep inside and restore.

Too Many To Mention

Although I said I would mention some of the most difficult forms of betrayal, the truth is that all betrayal is painful. You could have had your confidence broken by a prayer partner or the credit for a great idea stolen by a coworker. You may have been bullied by a teacher or betrayed by your boss who took the rewards owed to you. If you have been betrayed in any way, the Lord wants to heal your heart.

Lasting Damage

"I don't want to trust leaders anymore!" I cried to the Lord with tears streaming down my face. My husband and I were in the thick of a storm which led to several leaders leaving our church. The lady at the center was dear to my heart and the breakdown in our relationship was terribly painful. My heart's cry ascended again: "Lord, I just don't want to trust again!" I knew enough about the heart to know that my cry was not okay. Proverbs 3:5 says, "Trust in the Lord with all your heart, and lean not on your own understanding." Trusting God means I must be willing to trust His people. I continued in prayer and shared the pain of what felt to me like a very personal betrayal: "This hurts Lord, this is awful Lord..." I wept as my Heavenly Father healed my heart. Within a few moments of releasing my pain, I was ready to trust again.

The list of symptoms I shared in chapter 4 are all related to three underlying issues. When you deal with these three, your symptoms will gradually vanish. These three are pain, trust issues, and the fear of history repeating itself. The enemy doesn't mind if you get back up and continue serving as long as you still suffer from some crippling heart issues. We will diffuse the devil's plans to hamper your life by dealing with these hidden problems.

1. The Problem With Pain

There are countless brands of pain killers on the shelves of pharmacists. All sorts of things can cause pain: dehydration can give you a headache, falling can result in bruises, flu can give you a sore throat, decay can produce toothache, overdoing it at the gym can make your muscles hurt. You may be like many others and reach for Tylenol at the first twinge of pain. Then there is emotional pain: being overlooked for a promotion causes disappointment, a public put down makes you feel ashamed, mean words at home make you feel small, repeated delays make you feel discouraged. Perhaps you try to distract yourself, meet up with a friend to cheer yourself up, or perhaps you try to forget what happened. Because pain is inevitable, we think we must put up with it or find a quick fix. But just as Tylenol won't deal with tooth decay, distraction won't make emotional pain go away.

If you ignore pain, it won't disappear, it will just sink to the bottom of your soul. Buried in your heart, you probably won't be aware of it unless you see a reminder of what you went through. Then you may feel distressed and perhaps you will try to avoid circumstances that remind you of the discomfort. That's one of the ways the enemy seeks to influence your decisions. He causes you to be comfortable so that you will avoid certain people or places. But Romans 8:14 tells us that the children of God should be led by the Holy Spirit, not pushed in certain directions by past pain.

This is why is it vital that we develop a zero-tolerance attitude towards emotional pain. Proverbs 4:23 (NLT) underlines the importance of dealing with your pain: "Guard your heart above all else, for it determines the course of your life." The same verse in The Passion Translation says, "So above all, guard the affections of your heart, for they affect all that you are..." The Lord never wants you to ignore pain, He wants you to "... remove sorrow from your heart..." (Ecclesiastes 11:10a)

2. The Trouble With Trust Issues

The enemy wants to cause lasting damage to God's people when they have been hurt. Depending on the nature of the wound, the devil has a demonic plan he will attempt to execute. After bereavement, satan seeks to keep you weighed down with heaviness. After enduring terrible injustice, he wants you to be bitter. After betrayal, the enemy wants you to stop trusting, or at least become very wary.

Trust is vital. It is the atmosphere where your faith grows, and it is the cement that holds destiny relationships together. Proverbs 3:5 (AMP) says, "Lean on, trust in, and be confident in the Lord with all your heart and mind and do not rely on your own insight or understanding." After betrayal, the enemy tries to make your own understanding sound like wisdom. In contrast, the Lord asks us to utterly trust Him. When I'm not trusting God, I am by definition trusting in my own insight instead. I am relying on my opinions. Unfortunately, Proverbs 28:26s says, "He who trusts in his own heart is a fool, but whoever walks wisely will be delivered." Wisdom comes from trusting God, wariness comes from listening to our own assessments. Wisdom is outward looking, wariness is rooted in self-protection.

People often suggest that they trust God, they just don't trust people. But if I trust God, *then* I will be able to trust His people. Betrayal is one of the main ways the devil tries to stop you from trusting God and His people. Yes, trusting may be a risk, but the rewards are great. And once you know how to be healed any time you are betrayed, any possible sting in the tail of trust is removed.

3. The Fear Of History Repeating Itself

You may have already received a great deal of healing. However, one problem that many face as they are being restored is the fear of history repeating itself. You could be doing great, but if you see someone behaving in ways that remind you of past hurts, walls go up or anxiety builds. You might even label your reactions as discernment or a sixth sense. Unfortunately, if people's attitudes, comments or habits can trigger a strong reaction, this is a sign that fear of the past being repeated is controlling you. When anxiety or alarm dictate our decisions, we are being led about by old pain. The Lord wants to deal with any angst or nervousness that creeps in when you see certain signs. He wants to silence fear's whispers so that you can hear the voice of the Holy Spirit. You can enjoy perfect peace and complete confidence when the Lord is directing all your decisions.

In the next chapter, we will look at how you can be fully restored by the Lord. He is able to uproot all lasting damage caused by betrayal so that you can live the abundant life that Jesus died to provide. Before we close this chapter, we will bring our pain and fear to the Lord in prayer.

Heavenly Father,

As I have read, I have been brought back to times when my trust has been broken and it hurt me deeply. What happened wasn't right and it wasn't fair, and it shattered something inside. (*Now tell the Lord exactly what you went through. Explain what happened and how it made you feel. Talk to your Wonderful Counsellor in as much detail as possible.*) I realize now that I have been afraid of reliving the pain of the past in new relationships. I have been wary of anything that even slightly reminded me of what I suffered.

I ask You to reach into the depths of my heart and take my pain away. I give You my hurts as an offering. I don't want to keep this pain, so I ask You to take it away. I don't want to be influenced by fear, I desire to be led by Your Spirit. So Lord, I invite You to do a deep work in my heart and life. Take complete control of my decisions. I surrender afresh to You, Oh Lord.

I ask You to fill my heart afresh with Your precious Spirit. I receive Your tender love into the depths of my soul. Thank You for your wonderful healing. You are so kind to me. Now I ask You to seal where you have started to heal.

In Jesus' name I pray,

Amen.

Chapter 6

GOD'S PURPOSE

God always has a plan. When the original pathway that the Lord intended for your life is blocked, He reveals a divine alternative. Jeremiah 29:11 (NIV) speaks of plans in the plural because when Plan A is thwarted, Plan B, C or D kicks in: "For I know the plans I have for you," declares the Lord, "plans to prosper you and not to harm you, plans to give you hope and a future."

Your Heavenly Father has a way of bringing you through victorious, even after the worst betrayals. But He does not stop there! He is also able to turn the most terrible of situations around for your good. He can take the foul attacks of the enemy and do something wonderful. In Genesis 50:20, Joseph shared how God turned the enemy's plans for good: "But as for you, you meant evil against me; but God meant it for good, in order to bring it about as it is this day, to save many people alive." What the enemy meant for your harm, the Lord will work together for your benefit. If you seek restoration, the time will come when the devil regrets wounding you.

We discovered in the last chapter the ways that the enemy tries to cause lasting damage. For you to come out the other side stronger, happier and more successful than before, you need to be healed. In this chapter, we will unpack the steps to your freedom.

Face The Pain

When you trust someone, the expectation is that they will not let you down. Have you ever played team building games at work or church away days? There is an icebreaker that involves people dividing into twos. One of the pair stands behind their partner who is then asked to fall backwards. Of course, the one standing behind catches the one falling back. The point is that we fall back without being able to see the person standing behind us. It is designed to build trust in teams. If the catcher stepped out of the way and their partner crashed to the ground, it would be shocking and painful. It could cause serious injury. After such an experience, who would want to trust again?

In order to be healed of betrayal, it is vital that you face the shock and pain in the presence of God. I know it's distressing, but please don't turn away from your worst experiences, don't avoid looking at how horrible it all was. If there was a moment when it all began, please face that memory. Perhaps you came home to the reality of your spouse's unfaithfulness. Maybe a letter landed on your lap, or a photograph was brought to your attention. You could have gone through a slow burn betrayal where one thing after another came to light. Please don't try to keep these memories hidden in the dark corners of your heart. While they are buried, they will still have power in your life. If you don't look back, those recollections maintain their ability to control your reactions and decisions. When you face your pain, you start the process of breaking free from betrayal's power. But don't look back alone, deal with these painful moments in the presence of God.

The Importance Of Talking

Jesus is your Wonderful Counsellor (see Isaiah 9:6). Counselling only works when a client shares their difficulties with their counsellor from their heart. I encourage you to share your hurts with the One who is able to heal. Tell the Lord what you went through and how it made you feel. You do not need to sanitize your story for God. Tell Him how it really affected you. This is vital because there is a connection between your heart and your mouth. Luke 6:45b says, "...out of the abundance of the heart his mouth speaks." If you don't talk about your distress, it gets buried inside. When you talk to the Lord about the pain you have endured, you release toxic emotion trapped inside. You show your pain the exit!

God described King David as a man after His own heart (see Acts 13:22). He was a warrior and a worshipper, but he was also a talker. We see no evidence that David shared his pain with his close friends. However, we see numerous occasions in the Psalms when David told God how he felt in the midst of desperate circumstances. The man that God said was chasing His heart was utterly honest in prayer. Let's look at some examples of David telling the Lord about the pain of betrayal. Please understand that Psalms is more than a song book, it is also a prayer journal.

In Psalms 35:13-15 (TPT), David poured out his heart to God: "I even prayed over them when they were sick. I was burdened and bowed low with fasting and interceded for their healing, and I didn't stop praying. I grieved for them, heavyhearted, as though they were my dearest family members or my good friends who were sick, nearing death, needing prayer. But when I was the one who tripped up and stumbled, they came together to slander me, rejoicing in my time of trouble, tearing me to shreds with their lies and betrayal." David did not say, "Lord, I am going through a tough season." No! He shared in detail exactly what was causing him distress. He gave examples of why it felt so wrong. He expressed the depths of his pain, he held nothing back from God.

One of David's closest friends stabbed him in the back and deserted him in a time of great need. The king did not bury the sense of abandonment, he talked to his Wonderful Counsellor. In Psalms 41:9 (NLT), David shared his heart with the Lord: "Even my best friend, the one I trusted completely, the one who shared my food, has turned against me." He did not bottle his emotions, he shared his pain and disappointment with God.

There is another lesson we can learn from David's prayer life. He did not stop talking to God about a painful experience until his heart was free from all sadness. In Psalms 55:12-14 (NLT), he presented the betrayal of his friend to the Lord again: "It is not an enemy who taunts me—I could bear that. It is not my foes who so arrogantly insult me—I could have hidden from them. Instead, it is you—my equal, my companion and close friend. What good fellowship we once enjoyed as we walked together to the house of God." Then a third time, later in the same chapter, he talked to God. In Psalms 55:20-21 (NLT) he said: "As for my companion, he betrayed his friends; he broke his promises. His words are as smooth as butter, but in his heart is war. His words are as soothing as lotion, but underneath are daggers!" David did not internalize his shock, he brought each aspect of the experience to his Heavenly Father. He talked to the Lord until the hurt was gone.

The Power Of Surrender

One of the ways that the enemy is able to keep us in pain is by causing us to hold on to our hurts. There is nothing about betrayal that is acceptable. It is cruel and unjust. When you've been betrayed, the enemy tries to use the sense of injustice to make you hold tightly to your pain. The devil will whisper lies into your ears suggesting that if you let go, the people who hurt you will not be held to account. The enemy will try to tell you that by holding on, you will protect yourself from falling for the same trick again. In reality, all that holding pain does is open the door to the spirit of heaviness and the root of bitterness. Both will cause even more harm.

After you have talked to the Lord about your distress and disappointment, it is vital that you surrender. Tell the Lord that you don't want to hold on to your hurts any longer. Lay your pain down at the feet of Jesus. Tell Him that you refuse to hold your hurts any longer, then ask Him to take them away. You may not have thought that your pain could be an offering, but let me tell you, when you have been wronged, laying it down is a sacrifice and I believe the Lord receives it as a sign of your love for Him and your trust in Him.

A Key To Your Freedom

Our lives must be built upon the Rock of Jesus Christ (see Matthew 7:24-26), but our growth is nurtured through our destiny connecting relationships. We see this pattern throughout Scripture.ABraham could only become the father of faith by waiting for his wife Sarah to conceive. Esther needed the wisdom of her cousin Mordecai to prepare for her purpose. Elisha had to serve Elijah (even when he rejected him) to receive the prophetic mantle. David needed the correction of Nathan to rescue his relationship with God. Paul the apostle needed the companionship of Timothy and Titus, while they needed his fatherly guidance. You and I also need our destiny helpers, but they are the very relationships that the devil targets.

Every one of us makes mistakes, and sometimes our shortcomings wound others. Just as you will inevitably have hurt others, even your most loyal companions may let you down. We have to know how to let go of wrongdoing to ensure we come out the other side of every relationship disappointment. "Our struggle is not against flesh and blood…" (Ephesians 6:12 NIV) as the enemy would have us believe. We need to be more determined than the devil and willing to do what it takes to defuse betrayal's power. It is vital that you forgive anyone who has betrayed your trust. We don't always know who is linked to our future, so we must work overtime to keep our hearts free.

One problem is that you may think you have forgiven, when you actually haven't. Matthew 18:35 (NIV) says, "… forgive your brother or sister from your heart…" One of the ways you can be sure that you have fully forgiven is that you can pass what I call

'The Smile Test'. Close your eyes and picture the face of the person who betrayed you the most. Can you smile kindly at their reflection in your thoughts? Is your heart tender towards them? Until you and I can pass The Smile Test, we need to pursue forgiveness.

Joseph's Route To Promotion

God had huge plans for Joseph. Let me pause for a moment to make an important statement. True joy comes from fulfilling your purpose. Outside of God's perfect will for your life, you will always feel frustrated or somewhat disappointed. The Lord has a tremendous plan for you that will bring you great joy. God also had a phenomenal future in store for Joseph. As a teenager, Joseph dreamt of greatness and knew that the Lord had an exciting future in store for him.

However, at just 17 years of age, Joseph was betrayed. He was beaten, stripped, and then sold to human traffickers. The perpetrators told his dad – Joseph's only living parent – that he was dead. As a vulnerable teenager, Joseph was cut off from his family and everything he knew. He was bought by slave traders, probably transported naked in chains across the desert, then sold like a lump of meat to a slave owner in Egypt. Who were the perpetrators of this heinous crime? His own brothers.

When the ones you love shatter your trust, it can be soul destroying. You may have been abandoned, attacked, or abused by your own family. You could have been the victim of unfaithfulness or cruelty, you could have been rejected or cut off. When the damage done is devastating, it can make forgiveness feel almost impossible. That's why I'm grateful for the example of Joseph. You cannot weep while you hug your perpetrator unless you have let go of their offenses. Joseph cried and embraced his brothers when they were reunited. How did he forgive the men who tried to destroy him, the men who sold him, and cut him off from his father and his family?

The greatest insight into the thoughts of Joseph's heart probably comes from his words to his brothers in Genesis 50:18-21: "Then his brothers also went and fell down before his face, and they said, "Behold, we are your servants." Let me pause to ask you a question. Have you ever imagined a moment when you could address those who wronged you from a position of power? Have you seen yourself putting them in their place and making them squirm? Joseph had the power to make his brothers' lives miserable. He could have met their physical needs while constantly reminding them that they owed him everything. This was payback time for Joseph's brothers.

However, let's listen to our hero's response to his brothers who were pleading for mercy in Genesis 50:19-21: "Joseph said to them, "Do not be afraid, for am I in the place of God? But as for you, you meant evil against me; but God meant it for good, in order to bring it about as it is this day, to save many people alive. Now therefore, do not be afraid; I will provide for you and your little ones." And he comforted them and spoke kindly to them."

When Joseph had the chance to condemn his brothers, he showed kindness instead. For me, the most powerful statement he made was this: "...am I in the place of God?..." (Genesis 50:19b) Joseph refused to hold anything against them because he recognized that unforgiveness is built upon judgement. If I hold something against someone, I have not only judged their actions to be wrong, but I have also judged *them* to be wrong. I have acted as judge. With his statement, Joseph was saying, only God has the right to judge you, and I am not God.

I don't know what you have been through, but I do know that holding onto anger will harm you, not the people who made your life miserable. Resentment eats us up inside and eventually destroys our souls (see Job 5:2). Bitterness poisons our hearts and ultimately disqualifies us from the favor of God (see Acts 8:23 and Hebrews 12:15). No wonder the devil works overtime to feed thoughts that fuel anger and offense. Unforgiveness binds you to your pain and to the people of the past. When you let go of what a person did to hurt you, you also let go of them, and walk into freedom.

You Can Trust God

It is vital after we have been betrayed that we choose to trust again. The enemy wants you to be isolated by suspicion. We don't trust people because they are perfect, we trust people because we trust God to take care of us. The restoration of your ability to believe others begins with replacing your trust in the Lord. Let's look again at Proverbs 3:5 (AMP): "Lean on, trust in, and be confident in the Lord with all your heart and mind and do not rely on your own insight or understanding." It's time to take your eyes off the fallibility of people and instead look to the faithfulness of God.

Throughout the psalms, King David repeatedly made statements like this: "O Lord my God, in You I put my trust..." (Psalms 7:1a) After David went through betrayals, he got into God's presence and replaced his trust in Him. Trust is not a one-time decision. Any time our perspective of people has been shaken, we need to go back to God and put our trust in Him. Once your heart is safe in His hands again, you can start to trust others. Although we are required as Christians to forgive, trust is optional. However, we can't grow into our purpose and fulfill our destiny unless we trust people. We trust others because we trust God. We trust others knowing that any time we are let down, the Lord will restore.

Paul's Perspective

Should we trust the people who betrayed us? When it became clear that The Berlin Wall was going to come down, the American State Department and the CIA found themselves in uncharted waters. What should they do if suddenly Russian swords were actually being turned into plough shares? A new policy emerged in how to treat the new hands of friendship which were being extended across what was an iron curtain. 'Trust But Verify' became the new policy mantra in America. It became a slogan in many walks of life.

What relevance does this have in a chapter about betrayal? A common question people ask when the person who caused the pain is still around is; "How can you ever trust that person again?" My answer is usually, 'Trust But Verify'. Although I'm using the American Government's language, like most enduring wisdom, this principle is Biblical. After being terribly betrayed by his brothers, Joseph fully forgave them all, providing food for them and their families. However, before Joseph invited them to enjoy the privileges of living with him in Egypt, he tested his brothers' characters. Once he could see that they had changed, he opened up the best of the land to them and their families.

Restoration Time

Talking to the Lord about your ordeal, surrendering your pain as a sacrifice, and letting go of any anger pave the way for restoration. Psalms 147:3 (TPT) promises, "He heals the wounds of every shattered heart." There is no wound caused by betrayal that the Lord can't completely heal. Jesus died on the cross so that you could be made whole, even after terrible experiences. He literally carried your hurts and felt your agony so that you could be restored. Isaiah 53:4a says, "Surely He has borne our griefs and carried our sorrows…" The next verse goes on to say: "… with the stripes [that wounded] Him we are healed and made whole." (Isaiah 53:5b AMP)

Healing is just the first part of God's plan of restitution. When He heals, God takes your pain away, but restoration is when you are recompensed. The Lord wants you to benefit somehow from the trouble that the enemy intended for your harm. Let's look again at the truths that Joseph shared with his brothers in Genesis 50:20:

"But as for you, you meant evil against me; but God meant it for good, in order to bring it about as it is this day, to save many people alive."

It is obvious from Joseph's emotional liberty and joy that his heart was healed. But God did not stop there. The Lord used betrayal as Joseph's transport system to get him to the place where he would be promoted to the position of Prime Minister. God then used our hero to save thousands of Egyptians, as well as his own family, from starvation during famine. One of the men who was preserved through Joseph's ministry was his brother Judah – who was carrying the seed of Jesus Christ. The devil probably thought he had destroyed Joseph, but the Lord brought untold good out of terrible betrayal.

2 Corinthians 1:3-4 (TPT) says, "All praises belong to the God and Father of our Lord Jesus Christ. For he is the Father of tender mercy and the God of endless comfort. He always comes alongside us to comfort us in every suffering so that we can come alongside those who are in any painful trial. We can bring them this same comfort that God has poured out upon us." The Lord can use your journey of restoration to bring healing to others. If you fix your faith on God's ability to turn your pain around for good, you will see His hand at work in marvelous ways.

As we draw this chapter to a close, let's prepare our hearts to pray. Proverbs 20:27 reveals God's desire to uncover buried pain that has been weighing you down: "The spirit of a man is the lamp of the Lord, searching all the inner depths of his heart." Let's begin our time of prayer by asking the Lord to highlight hidden hurts so that we can be healed.

Heavenly Father,

I open my heart to You, I ask You to shine Your light into the depths of my soul. Reveal buried pain, Lord. I don't want to be weighed down by these hurts and wounds anymore. I surrender all my sadness to You Lord. I won't hold onto my pain any longer, I am ready to be healed, I want to be free.

Lord, You know what I have been through. I had my heart shattered by people that I believed loved me. I have felt the deep pain of betrayal and it hurt me badly. It was so wrong and what they did was cruel, Lord. I felt torn apart by their words and actions. (*Now tell the Lord exactly what happened. Talk to your Wonderful Counsellor. Share your hurtful experiences with Him, explain what you went through and tell Him how it made you feel. Please don't hold back. He is by your side, He wants to hear you share from your heart.*)

It hurt, Lord. They broke my heart and shattered my trust. But I don't want to hold on to their offenses anymore. I choose today to forgive from my heart because You always forgive me. I choose today to cancel their debt. Lord, I forgive _____ (insert their names). I forgive _____ for (*now tell the Lord what they did to hurt you and give Jesus each offense, one by one.*) I let go of their wrongs, I cancel their debt. _____ you don't owe me anything anymore. I let it go, it's over! (*If they are still alive, continue*): Lord, I ask You to bless _____. Bless their family and their livelihood, I pray. I am free!

Lord, I ask You to heal me in every place where I have been hurt. I ask You to restore me deep inside. Please fill my heart with Your healing balm. I receive Your wonderful love in the depths of my heart. Where you have healed, please now seal what You have done. I receive Your peace.

Now Lord, I make a decision to trust again. I open my heart afresh to You and I put my trust in You. Because I trust you, I can trust others. Thank You Lord that you will take care of me any time I am let down. I rely entirely on You Lord. Thank You that as I trust others, I will enjoy rewarding relationships. Please give me wisdom and understanding, please lead me by Your Spirit into Your will for my life. I refuse to be suspicious and instead I choose to believe the best in those You have brought into my life. Thank You for protecting me and guiding me every day of my life.

I give You all the glory and praise for restoring my soul and my life.

In Jesus' mighty name I pray,

Amen.

Part Three
CRISIS

"An appalling and horrible thing [bringing desolation and destruction] has come to pass…" Jeremiah 5:30 (AMP)

Chapter 7

THE PAIN OF CRISIS

"Come, now!" the doctor blurted with a grave sense of urgency. We were ushered into a makeshift emergency room where a big team of medics was working on our daughter's tiny frame. "She's had a third cardiac arrest," he stated, "We are doing everything we can." My husband and I prayed as we paced the floor. Naomi was hooked up to a web of wires and wrapped up in an aluminum blanket. Our princess was fighting for her life.

I will never forget the moment when the atmosphere changed. The alarm dulled as clinicians began withdrawing from her bedside. With immense sensitively, one by one, doctors quietly left the room. Soon only four remained. The lead consultant looked up at my husband and me: "We usually attempt to resuscitate an adult for 25 minutes and a child for ten minutes. We have been trying to restart your daughter's heart for 25 minutes. There is nothing more that we can do." In one surreal statement, life as we knew it crashed to an end. Our daughter was with us one moment and gone the next. Her killer was meningitis.

Usually a happy, healthy little girl, Naomi was our only child when she died. She had bright blue eyes, blonde curly hair and an irresistible giggle. Her name, which means 'our delight', aptly described our love for our sweet daughter. At the time of this tragedy, my husband and I were pastoring our small but growing church in London, England. We were serving God with all of our hearts and doing our best to lead His people. How would we make it out the other side?

It's Not New

While living rough in the wilderness, David wrote, "For innumerable evils have surrounded me… so that I am not able to look up; they are more than the hairs of my head; therefore my heart fails me." (Psalms 40:12). David felt surrounded by suffering to the extent that his heart was breaking under the strain. If you have visited "the valley of the shadow of death" described in Psalm 23:4 (you may even be in that desolate place right now), please know that you are not alone. Many of our Bible heroes have experienced painful tragedies.

- Adam and Eve endured the agony of knowing that one of their sons, Cain, murdered his brother, their other son Abel. It must have felt like both sons' lives were extinguished in one senseless act of violence.

- Noah must have shuddered to the core as he heard thunderous rains flood the earth, destroying the men and women that he had lived among and preached to for years. From safe inside the ark, he probably heard their screams and cries.

- For nearly two decades, Jacob lived with the pain of believing Joseph, his favorite son, was torn to pieces by wild beasts, then lived his latter days knowing his family had deceived him.

- The man who carried the seed of Jesus Christ, Judah, suffered the almost unbearable tragedy of losing two sons and his wife.

- Moses was despised and rejected by the people he was called to lead, forcing him to escape to the wilderness where he lived for the next 40 years.

- Hosea lived with the constant unfaithfulness of his wife.

- Job's businesses failed, his children died in a freak accident, his health failed, his marriage was in crisis, and his reputation was ruined.

- Esther's parents died when she was a child, so from a young age, she was raised by her cousin Mordecai.

- Naomi lost her husband Elimelech while the family was living in a foreign country. As though that wasn't enough pain for one woman to bear, both her sons, Mahlon and Chilion, also died.

There are so many more examples we could look at in this broken world. It is really important to realize that while we live in a fallen world, awful things will happen. Job 5:7 says, "Yet man is born to trouble, as the sparks fly upward." The word for trouble is âmâl. Among other things, it means misery, pain, sorrow, and toil. If you watch an electrician drilling, you will notice that sparks always rise. In the same way, it is inevitable that you and I will experience pressure and pain. I don't know what calamity you have already endured. Your marriage could have suddenly collapsed. Your ministry may have gone through a terrible shaking. You could have been made redundant or filed for bankruptcy. You might have lost someone you dearly loved. The question is not, 'Will we face crisis?', but rather, 'How can we come out the other side strong?'

Specialist In Impossibilities

Our lives crashed when our daughter died. It felt like the end of the world, and I had no idea how we would come out the other side, or even if there was another side. We lost our precious princess, and we lost our role as parents. The void Naomi left behind was huge and the pain was almost unbearable. Maybe you have suffered a terrible loss that has left an emptiness in your life. It is in these moments that we must settle some things. God never has been and never will be the author of sickness. He did not take our daughter away and He has not caused your pain either, that was the work of the devil. I am grateful that I knew this to be true. I did battle with tormenting questions which I will tackle in chapter 8, but I never saw God as the author of our suffering. When we see God as the problem, it is difficult to turn to Him for help, and believe me when I say, He is the only One who can bring lasting restoration.

About a month after Naomi left the earth, I decided it was time to tidy away her toys. Home alone, I found a bag and started to fill it with our daughter's favorite things. When I picked up her little toy telephone, I broke. Just ten days before she passed away, I took some photographs of our little girl for my office. She posed for me, pretending to be making calls like her mommy. An avalanche of pain flooded my soul as I held that little phone in my hands. I did not know what to do with the agony. I had no eloquent, faith filled prayers. Instead, I cried out with all my might to my Heavenly Father: "HELP!"

King David did the same in times of agony. In Psalms 18:6 (NLT) we read, "But in my distress I cried out to the Lord; yes, I prayed to my God for help. He heard me from his sanctuary; my cry to him reached his ears." God heard David, He heard me, and He hears you when you cry out for His help. Almost immediately after I called to the Lord, I felt His hand reach down from heaven into the depths of my heart. God literally pulled pain out of me. It was a powerful experience that produced an astonishing depth of relief. Afterwards, I sat on our sofa exhausted but amazed. That was the beginning of my healing journey.

Just as the Lord healed my brokenness, He can restore you, too. Psalms 147:3 (TPT) says, "He heals the wounds of every shattered heart." There is no pain that is too terrible for our Heavenly Father. He can heal you anywhere you have been hurt. After our daughter died, my husband and I both began a healing journey. Some moments of restoration were supernatural like the one I have just described. On other occasions, relief came by talking to our Wonderful Counsellor (see Isaiah 9:6).

Better Out Than In

I will repeat a vital principle that is a key to your healing. You and I have been designed with a connection between our hearts and our mouths. Matthew 12:34b says, "...out of the abundance of the heart the mouth speaks." When you don't talk, pain gets trapped inside, bound up by unspoken words. When you share how you feel, you release distress. Talking with a friend will help, but speaking freely about your pain with God will bring real relief. Jeremiah understood the importance of talking to the Lord. In Lamentations 2:19a, he wrote, "Arise, cry out in the night... pour out your heart like water before the face of the Lord..." When we pour out our hearts to a friend, we share our deepest concerns. This verse encourages you and me to talk openly to our Heavenly Father about our distress. God treasures moments when you share your heart with Him.

During our time of grief, I instinctively knew that my pain was better out than in. Any time sadness surfaced, I did not push it down. Wherever I was, I would steal myself away and get alone. At work, I would head to a secret corridor; at friends' houses, I would go the bathroom; at church, I would find a quiet space. When grief overwhelmed me, I would get alone with God for a few moments and let myself cry. I did not subdue the pain. After releasing any tears, I would tell Him what was hurting me the most in that moment. Afterwards, I would powder my nose and get on with my day. Through a mix of healing encounters and talking to my Wonderful Counsellor, God restored my soul. Minus the makeup, my husband tells a similar story. What the Lord did for us, He will do for you.

The Cruel Reality Of Crisis

The dictionary defines crisis as dramatic emotional upheaval. Having suffered the grief of 'losing' his favorite son Joseph, Jacob could not imagine enduring more pain. When his older sons wanted to bring his youngest Benjamin to Egypt, Jacob responded:

"But if you take this one also from me, and calamity befalls him, you shall bring down my gray hair with sorrow to the grave." (Genesis 44:29). Jacob was explaining that if anything happened to Benjamin, he would lose the will to live. He said that he could not take any more of this type of pain.

The sorrow of a crisis can be so heavy that it can cause something to die inside. It opens the door to a deluge of sadness that can feel overwhelming. Calamity is an old-fashioned word which means a great misfortune or disaster, grievous affliction, adversity, or misery. Calamity is usually unexpected, even shocking. A broken marriage, the untimely death of a loved one, a failed ministry, a family tragedy, bankruptcy, or devastated dreams – all these are examples. I don't know what you have gone through, but I do know that it is probably impossible to go through life without experiencing great pain.

Before we go any further, let's look at the nature of the human soul. Your heart is your most valuable possession because it decides how your life turns out. Proverbs 4:23 (NLT) explains: "Guard your heart above all else, for it determines the course of your life." Your heart is also sensitive. This is because your soul was made in the image of God's soul for the giving and receiving of love, and for fellowship. This means that it was made to be absorbent – able to soak up the very atmosphere of Eden: love and glory. So, as well as being valuable, your heart is vulnerable.

Finally, your heart can lie. Jeremiah 17:9 (AMP) says, "The heart is deceitful above all things... Who can know it [perceive, understand, be acquainted with his own heart and mind]?" We think we know ourselves, but we don't. Our hearts tell us that all is well when all is not well. Sometimes the truth is painful, so our default is to look away. The Lord knows your heart and wants to search your soul to reveal hidden pain that has been weighing you down. Let's pause for a moment and ask the Lord to shine His light into our souls.

Heavenly Father,

I open my heart to You. I don't know which hurtful memories are locked away in the caverns of my soul, secretly influencing my life. I don't want hidden hurts to hold me back any longer, so I ask You to shine Your light into the depths of my heart. Reveal buried pain that has been hampering my progress; reveal so that I may be healed, Lord.

In Jesus' name I pray,

Amen.

Crisis comes in different shapes and sizes, but please don't compare your pain with the experiences of others. It's not what happened that matters, but how much it hurt. Try not to dismiss something you have gone through as unimportant just because you know someone who went through a more dramatic tragedy. Equally, it's not helpful to see your story as the worst. The former may cause you to underplay the pain. The latter may trap you in the lie that God can't help. Your Heavenly Father is the Master Restorer.

After our daughter died, people told us that we would never get over such a loss. Some told us the pain would reduce with time, but that we would always feel Naomi's absence. Medics, fellow ministers and friends seemed to agree: you will carry sadness to the grave. But our loving God had a different perspective. Unmoved by our broken state, He accepted every one of our invitations to heal our hearts. Again and again, the Lord reached into the depths of our pain and restored our souls. Isaiah 53:4 says, "Surely He has borne our griefs and carried our sorrows…" Jesus died on the cross for more than just our sin, He also carried our pain. The Lord suffered to make you and me whole.

The Brutality Of Shock

"A horrible and shocking thing has happened…" (Jeremiah 5:30, NLT). Shock may sound harmless, but please don't underestimate its impact. Shock comes like a punch in the guts and can cause even strong people to be shaken to the core. Some of the Bible's greatest leaders experienced its force: "... I, Daniel, was in shock. I was like a man who had seen a ghost..." (Daniel 7:28, MSG). Your chest might have become tight, or your mind foggy. Your stomach could have crunched, or you may have been faint. You could have felt disconnected from what happened, like you were watching a movie of events unfolding. Perhaps you experienced intense anger, feeling the need to scream, or maybe everything inside of you wanted to run from the situation.

Tragedy, by definition, is heartbreaking. But when it is a bolt out of the blue, the impact can be even more ferocious. Perhaps you were at ease, certain that everything would work out, and then suddenly, everything fell apart around you. 1 Thessalonians 5:3 says, "...they say, "Peace and safety!" then sudden destruction comes upon them, as labor pains upon a pregnant woman..." Although I had attended classes and heard stories about giving birth, I was not really prepared for the agony or the intensity. Like many women, I was overwhelmed. The verse above explains that tragedy is similar, but without a precious child to soothe your soul.

You may feel traumatized by your memories. Job 21:6 (MSG) says, "When I look back, I go into shock, my body is racked with spasms." If reminders of what you went through make you upset or anxious, the Lord wants to restore your soul. Any recollection from your life that still causes pain or dread is a memory that the Lord wants to heal. As shock evaporates, it often leaves behind a deadness on the inside. You may be living under a cloud of bewilderment. You could struggle to regain your zeal for life. When the shock and trauma are healed, you will be able to enjoy yourself again.

Secondhand Trauma

Secondhand trauma is when you witness someone else suffer. Because the difficulty didn't happen to you, you may dismiss the impact. But secondhand pain is real. Genesis 34:7 (NLT) says,

"Meanwhile, Jacob's sons had come in from the field as soon as they heard what had happened. They were shocked and furious that their sister had been raped..." Jacob's sons dearly loved their sister Dinah, so they were devastated at the horrific news that she had been raped. If we don't deal with shock, it can drive us to make disastrous decisions. Simeon and Levi ended up murdering the men who defiled their sister and as a result, their father withheld his blessing. Simeon never fully recovered.

Ezra was a national leader that was knocked sideways by shock. It was not Ezra's experiences that winded him, he was shattered by news of the behavior of the children of Israel. "When I heard this, I tore my cloak and my shirt, pulled hair from my head and beard, and sat down utterly shocked." (Ezra 9:3 NLT). I have seen dads and moms cut to the heart by their children's ungodly decisions. Maybe you saw the call of God on your child's life while they were growing up. Perhaps they loved the Lord as a young person, then deserted their faith. You may wonder what went wrong, you could blame yourself. The truth is that watching someone you love turn their back on God can be mortifying.

In order to pray in faith about a situation, your heart needs to be free from debilitating emotions. Faith is incubated in your heart as Romans 10:10a explains: "For with the heart one believes..." If your heart is weighed down with grief or if you have been shaken by news, it will be difficult to be full of faith. In fact, it is virtually impossible for discouragement and faith to cohabit in your heart. You need to release your distress so that you can pray with expectation. You need to go back to the place of pain in order to leave tragedy behind you permanently.

Leading Through Personal Crisis

"Elisha saw it and cried out, "My father! My father! ...Elisha tore his clothes in distress. Elisha picked up Elijah's cloak, which had fallen when he was taken up. Then Elisha returned to the bank of the Jordan River." (2 Kings 2:12-13, NLT) There is something about the finality of death that is brutal. Elijah was Elisha's spiritual father and mentor. They had been together for quite some time. Yes, Elisha knew Elijah was going to glory, but knowledge that the end is imminent does not take away the pain of irreversible separation. In the midst of distress, Elisha had to pick up his mentor's mantle and pursue his ministry. He demonstrated great courage even though his heart was hurting.

If you're a parent, a pastor, or a leader, you will have to stay at the helm in the midst of personal trials. The pastor of Bethel Church in Redding, California demonstrated remarkable courage and strength after his wife died. Four days after she went to glory, Bill Johnson preached one of the best messages I have ever heard. I remember hearing him say something like this, "God does not owe me an explanation, I owe Him my worship." Bill Johnson modelled leading through tragedy with remarkable dignity. He showed the world how we can honor the Lord, even in the midst of a heartbreaking crisis.

I was getting ready to teach at Life Changers Bible Academy when the call came: "Mom's heart has stopped beating!" Prophet Cathy wasn't just my mentor, she was my beloved spiritual mom. We talked by text four or five times a week and I saw her about ten times a year, even though she lived in Florida. Nobody loved me the way she did. The news of her passing stabbed my heart. Stunned, I sat for a few minutes. I then pulled myself together and set off for church. I didn't bury the pain, I just forced my attention away from my sadness and onto the task at hand: a room full of students were hungry for the Word of God. I got myself to church, taught two sessions and prayed for our students.

Freely You Have Received

With ministry commitments fulfilled, I returned home to an empty house. I was relieved to have time alone. Early that evening, a surge of pain threw me to my knees. Crying from the depths of my heart, I poured out my anguish. I must have howled for twenty or thirty minutes as I told the Lord how much I loved that precious lady. Afterwards, I felt raw and empty, but I knew my healing had begun. Due to minister the following day twice at church, I sat quietly with my Bible open, listening to the Lord. That night I slept peacefully. Early the next morning I walked my dog through beautiful countryside. Tears trickled down my cheeks as I shared more sadness with my Heavenly Father. While I prayed, His healing love filled my soul. I was ready to minister.

Matthew 10:8b says, "...Freely you have received, freely give." Out of the overflow of two precious encounters, I was able to minister hope and healing to our people. Prophet Cathy was not just my spiritual mother, she was also the 'Mom of our House'. Bread is tastiest when it is just out of the oven and a healing anointing is most precious when it is flows straight from our hearts to others. "He always comes alongside us to comfort us in every suffering so that we can come alongside those who are in any painful trial. We can bring them this same comfort that God has poured out upon us." (2 Corinthians 1:4, TPT). God doesn't waste time, as soon as we bring our pain to Him, He will use our healing for His purposes.

Has the Lord brought any pain to the surface while you have been reading? You may be navigating a horrible family situation. Perhaps there has been a disaster at work, at church, or at home. You could have lost someone you love. It doesn't matter how long ago they passed away, if it still hurts, you still need to be healed. You may have witnessed someone fall apart or seen a shocking sight. Perhaps you have gone through some other type of crisis. Whatever you have suffered, the Lord wants to relieve your distress and heal your heart. Let's pray.

Heavenly Father,

I don't want to hold onto this pain any longer. I don't want buried shock to influence my decisions anymore, so I ask You to take me on a journey to restoration. I open my heart to You today, I won't push down my pain any longer. I bring the distressing experiences of my life to You Lord. (*Now tell God about any memory that has surfaced. Tell Him what happened and how you felt. Share what you went through in as much detail as possible. Talk to Him as your Wonderful Counsellor. If you suffered shock, tell Him how it made you feel, tell the Lord about every detail that comes to mind.*)

I ask You to heal my heart, O Lord. I give You my pain, I give You my distress, and I ask You to pour Your wonderful healing love into my heart. Fill my soul afresh with Your Spirit, I pray. I receive Your perfect peace.

In Jesus' name I pray,

Amen.

Chapter 8

SATAN'S PLAN

Calamity usually hits suddenly. Even a strong person can be floored by the force of shock. It can feel as though there is no way out of the overwhelming pain. Proverbs 6:15 (AMP) expresses the impact: "Therefore upon him shall the crushing weight of calamity come suddenly; suddenly shall he be broken..." The Bible talks about times when things happen all of a sudden. We all long for the joy of sudden breakthroughs, but sudden disaster can feel catastrophic. When you are struck by a trauma that you did not see coming, the enemy will try to trap you in a dark place. He uses a host of foul ploys. Let's look at some of the most common.

A Permanent Location

Unfortunately, suffering is part of life. Almost all our Bible heroes endured great difficulties while they were alive. Job 5:7 states: "Yet man is born to trouble, as the sparks fly upward." Fierce trials are inevitable while we live in a broken, fallen world. However, bewilderment should never become our permanent location. Psalms 23:4 (AMP) explains, "Yes, though I walk *through* the [deep, sunless] valley of the shadow of death, I will fear or dread no evil, for You are with me; Your rod [to protect] and Your staff [to guide], they comfort me." We are to walk through, and not to, the wilderness. God always has a plan to bring us out of adversity and back into abundance. Our job is holding to that belief when we are in the middle of dreadful distress.

A few days after our daughter died, my husband remembers me saying, "My love, this tragedy will not destroy us." I don't recall making that statement, but I am grateful that I knew in the midst of our pain that we still had a future. I do remember repeatedly singing a song with these lyrics: "I have a future, God has a plan for me, of this I'm sure, of this I'm sure. Jesus, You're my firm foundation…" These words helped to keep my heart hopeful. The enemy wants you to think that there is no way out of your pain, that you will have to live with sadness for the rest of your days. The father of lies suggests that some experiences are so crushing that you will never fully recover.

Scripture tells an appalling story in the book of Matthew. Enraged with anger, Herod ordered the massacre of all boys in and around Bethlehem who were two years and under. I cannot imagine the horror and grief that must have struck that community. Families everywhere suffered not just the loss, but the senseless murder of their precious sons. The entire city must have been traumatized.

In the midst of this city-wide crisis, we hear one grieving mother's response. Matthew 2:18 says, "A voice was heard in Ramah, lamentation, weeping, and great mourning, Rachel weeping for her children, refusing to be comforted, because they are no more." This heartbroken woman refused to be comforted because there was nothing she could do to bring her boys back. A life marked by mourning seemed to be the only possible response, and restoration appeared to be impossible.

The enemy wants you to believe that your circumstances are too bad for you to ever fully recover. He wants to trap you in a wilderness where you live with your pain and believe a lesser life is your lot. Maybe a divorce shattered you. Perhaps the collapse of your ministry or business left you utterly bewildered. It could be that you had your life torn apart by trauma. Our faithful Heavenly

Father wants you to know that He still has a plan. Jeremiah 29:11 (NIV) is as true in the valley as it is on the mountaintop: "For I know the plans I have for you," declares the Lord, "plans to prosper you and not to harm you, plans to give you hope and a future." We don't always understand why we have to suffer, but many who have been shattered by tragedy can testify to the truth of Psalms 147:3 (AMP): "He heals the brokenhearted and binds up their wounds [curing their pains and their sorrows]." He does not only comfort, but He is also able to cure your pain.

Destructive Declarations

Words are powerful. Think about it, God created heaven and earth by speaking them into existence, then He made you and me in His image. That means our words are also powerful. Proverbs 18:21 (NLT) says, "The tongue can bring death or life; those who love to talk will reap the consequences." What we say affects how we think and how we feel. Jesus taught about the power of our words in Mark 11:23. And Job 22:28 (AMP) says, "You shall also decide and decree a thing, and it shall be established for you..."

One of the ways that the enemy tries to trap us in the middle of a crisis is by influencing our conversations. The devil wants you to make forceful statements like: "I'll never come through this", "I can't take any more pain", "This is too much to bear", or "Our lives have been ruined." Satan knows that if he can suck you into making destructive declarations, he can make your life even more difficult. In my book My Pretend Friend, I look at these types of statements, and explain why each is false. For now, let me just say that the Bible has a very different perspective, and the Bible is true.

After our daughter died, one of the statements I kept repeating was: "Losing a child is the worst. You are supposed to bury your parents," I would claim, "But no-one should ever bury their children." Saying that my situation was "the worst" only strengthened my turmoil. Ecclesiastes 5:6 says, "Do not let your mouth cause your flesh to sin, nor say before the messenger of God that it was an error. Why should

God be angry at your excuse and destroy the work of your hands?" My own words were holding me in gloom and making my pain even greater.

Not only that, but I was also falling into another trap: comparing my trial with the misfortune of others. When we suggest one type of trauma is worse than another, we can unwittingly box ourselves (and others) into an even darker place. It is futile and not based on Bible truth. Our focus should be on how we recover, not on how hard we have been hit. If you realize that you have been sucked into negativity, we will break the power of any destructive declarations that you have made as we pray at the end of this chapter. You can also start today to use your tongue to breathe life into your situation. You can choose words that pave the way out of difficulty and into restoration.

The Blame Game

Since sin entered the world in the garden of Eden, so did blame. Adam blamed Eve for eating the forbidden fruit, and Eve blamed the serpent. Blame points the finger at someone else. It is not merely an attempt to understand what went wrong, it is usually fueled by judgement, and all too often, it traps us in a dark place. It carries with it feelings of anger and injustice. The enemy wants you to channel your energy into holding someone responsible for your pain, so that you don't have the capacity to seek your healing. It may feel justifiable and even important. However, the blame game has no winners. When you have suffered, you need all the help you can get to recover. Blame will not bring you relief or restoration. It will trap you in remorse.

I encourage you to put your proverbial weapons down. Make a decision to stop searching for the culprit and instead seek your restoration. The Bible says that our struggle is not against flesh and blood, it is not with people. Lift up your eyes instead to the Lord. He is able to deliver you from all pain and confusion. Jesus left His home in heaven and died on the cross to heal your broken heart. He paid the price necessary to lift your heaviness, and even to turn your mourning into joy (see Isaiah 61:1-3).

The Dark Cloud Of Confusion

In the months after our daughter died, one question kept reverberating around my mind: 'Why?' My husband and I were serving God with all of our hearts, and we worked hard to protect our daughter with our faith and prayers. Not only that, but we also have a loving and faithful God who is able to heal every disease. So why did our daughter have to die? What did we do wrong? She was innocent so why did she pay such a high price? The torment was eating away at me.

Maybe you have battled with similar questions. Perhaps you cannot fathom what on earth you could have done to deserve such a painful situation. You could struggle with the injustice. It might be that someone you love endured too much. Why her? Why him? Why us? Jacob felt let down by his sons and uttered a similar sentiment in Genesis 43:6 "Why did you deal so wrongfully with me...?" Perhaps that's how you feel.

A few months before Naomi fell sick, the daughter of some dear friends was admitted to hospital in a critical and potentially life-threatening condition. As I prayed for their daughter while things were touch and go, the Lord gave me the exact date that she would be released from the hospital. I am so grateful that God healed that precious little girl. But His faithfulness to her amplified my confusion: why did our daughter die? These questions rattled around my mind constantly and left me feeling bewildered. I remember telling a friend, "When the Lord gives me some answers, maybe I can start to heal."

Nehemiah 4:8 (AMP) describes one of the enemy's plans in the midst of a crisis: "And they all plotted together to come and fight against Jerusalem, to injure and cause confusion..." Confusion is horrible. It drives away peace and clutters up your mind. It is distressing and makes life feel chaotic. The enemy uses crisis to cause bewilderment because no-one can move forward while they are tormented by unanswered questions. I was trapped in that state of confusion.

Clearing Away Mental Cobwebs

After a few weeks of being plagued by these thoughts, I heard a message shared by a lady who had suffered a tragedy. While I listened, I sensed the Lord ask me something in response to my questions: "Could I ever provide you with a good enough reason why your little girl had to die?" Gripped by the question, I soon realized that there was nothing that God could say that would make our tragedy acceptable. "No." I answered, "There is nothing that You could say that would be a good enough reason for the death of our precious princess." The Lord then showed me that my quest for answers was only trapping me in torment. While I sought a reason, I was being battered by confusion.

"Will you give Me your questions as an offering?" the Lord asked me. Feeling vulnerable, I got into the presence of God. Then, with tears trickling down my cheeks, I laid down my questions. "I give up why," I told the Lord, "I give up my right to an answer. I give You all my questions, I give You all this turbulence as an offering. I leave it in Your hands." As I came out of my prayer closet, I realized that a cobweb of confusion that had been wrapped around my mind had been wiped away. A heavy weight had lifted off my shoulders and I was free to receive my healing.

King David understood a powerful principle about sacrifice. He said in 2 Samuel 24:24 (AMP): "I will not offer burnt offerings to the Lord my God of that which costs me nothing…" Every now and again, we get the opportunity to give something to God that costs us a great deal. When we give out of love and obedience, our offering will touch the heart of God. It may be hard to lay down your questions. However, the truth is that they are only causing chaos and torment. Though giving God your questions may be a costly sacrifice, afterwards, you will feel like you have laid down a heavy burden.

There is a right time and a wrong time to ask questions. When you are safe out the other side of confusion and torment, you may find it helpful to seek some understanding. However, please wait until your heart is at peace.

Believing God's Your Problem

The Bible tells the story of a woman who suffered terrible loss. Naomi's painful journey is described in Ruth 1:3,5: "Then Elimelech, Naomi's husband, died; and she was left, and her two sons... Then both Mahlon and Chilion also died; so the woman survived her two sons and her husband." I cannot imagine the agony of losing every member of your immediate family. Naomi was not in her own country surrounded by friends when crisis hit, she was alone in a foreign country. When you go through difficulty, it is helpful to surround yourself with people of faith and love who will help you find your way out.

Naomi ended up believing a cruel lie. In Ruth 1:20b-21, she said: "Do not call me Naomi; call me Mara, for the Almighty has dealt very bitterly with me. I went out full, and the Lord has brought me home again empty. Why do you call me Naomi, since the Lord has testified against me, and the Almighty has afflicted me?"

In her grief, Naomi believed the lie that her tragedy was the doing of the Lord. Perhaps Naomi's husband was wrong to move his family from Bethlehem to Moab? He may have been motivated by fear of famine rather than the leading of the Holy Spirit. We don't know, but we do know that God did not hurt Naomi's husband or sons. God is not the author of sin or sickness. He did not cause Naomi's grief, that was the enemy, and He did not cause your pain either. Thinking that God is against you is hurtful, but it is also tragic. He loves you, He wants the best for you, and He is the only One who can really help.

Romans 8:28 (NASB) makes a powerful promise: "And we know that God causes all things to work together for good to those who love God, to those who are called according to His purpose." The Lord turned Naomi's situation around for good and He is ready to do the same for you. God is not your problem, He is the One who has a plan for your restoration.

Jesus Didn't Show Up

When you go through painful trials, the enemy wants you to believe that God was missing in action. When Jesus fell asleep on a boat in the middle of a terrible storm, His disciples interpreted His inaction as a lack of love. Mark 4:38 tells the story: "But He was in the stern, asleep on a pillow. And they awoke Him and said to Him, "Teacher, do You not care that we are perishing?" Maybe that's how you feel? Perhaps you assume that you suffered because God didn't intervene? It's okay to express your doubts, in fact, saying it out loud can bring release. At the same time, I want you to know that the Lord only wants the best for you. And even when you can't sense His presence, the Lord has never left your side. Jesus was at rest in the boat because He knew they would reach the other side. He knows you can come through too.

Two close friends of the Lord Jesus felt abandoned when their brother died. Martha and Mary asked Jesus to come when Lazarus fell sick, but He delayed. The ladies must have been talking because they both made the exact same statement to Jesus when they saw Him: "Lord, if You had been here, my brother would not have died." (John 11:21) This thought must have caused the sisters a great deal of pain. Maybe it made them doubt His affection. Perhaps they felt forgotten.

If you have battled with thoughts that the Lord doesn't care, I want to share the response of Jesus to the pain of Martha, Mary and their friends. Let's look at John 11:33: "...when Jesus saw her weeping, and the Jews who came with her weeping, He groaned in the spirit and was troubled." In the same verse, The Passion

Translation says that Jesus "...shuddered with emotion and was deeply moved with tenderness and compassion." It pained Him to see their pain because He loved them with all of His heart. In the same way, He watches over you with tenderness when you are wounded. Jesus cares more than you will ever know.

Listen to the way God feels when you are troubled. Jeremiah 8:21a says, "For the hurt of the daughter of my people I am hurt." It pains the Lord to see you wounded. Not only that, but He has also never left you and He never will (see Hebrews 13:5). Martha and Mary thought Jesus had deserted them because He didn't come the moment He heard that Lazarus was sick, but Jesus still had a plan. He had a different miracle for these precious sisters. I want you to know that God still has a plan for your life, and He has miracles for you in your future that you did not expect.

When our daughter died, I was devastated, I wondered where God had been in all of this. However, the reality was that the Lord stayed by my side every step of the way. The enemy may have won a battle, but God was about to win a war. The tragedy that the devil thought would destroy us led to a precious journey of restoration. God healed our broken hearts then gave us a ministry that punishes satan daily. He turned my river of pain into a healing spring that ministers to many. The death of our daughter led to the birth of our healing ministry. What the enemy meant for harm, the Lord turned around for the good of many (see Genesis 50:20). The following story is just one of countless examples. God wants to turn your pain around for good too.

Tragic Loss

Kate's son Ben died when he was just eight years old after a long battle with sickness. After he passed away, the Lord graciously gave this precious mom a vision of Ben in heaven which brought her a great deal of comfort. However, when Ben died, Kate felt like a part of her died too. She just wanted to be in heaven with her son, despite having a family that needed her on earth.

Two years after Kate's loss, she attended one of our conferences called Healed for Life.

"As I listened to Jo talk about the death of her daughter, I could not stop crying. Overwhelming grief welled up from the depths of my soul" Kate continued, "As I wept, the Lord did a supernatural work inside me, He restored the shattered places in my soul and healed my broken heart. God lifted a heavy weight of disappointment and oppression. I remember going to bed feeling an excitement and joy I had never before experienced! Before leaving that conference, the Lord showed me that just as an onion has layers, so my restoration would go deeper and deeper, one layer at a time."

After that first encounter, Kate continued attending our events and went on a wonderful healing journey. She explained, "Now when I look back, I no longer feel any grief. Instead, I have an immense sense of joy and gratitude. I am part of the Whole Heart Ministries team and have the privilege of helping others on their way to total restoration." What God did for Kate, He can do for you too.

The Fear Of Feeling The Pain Again

One of the ways the enemy tries to trap you in the past is by making you afraid of experiencing similar pain again. Fear is always a trap. Job 22:10 says, "Therefore snares are all around you, and sudden fear troubles you". If you worry that you will suffer the same again, you end up living with anxiety. Any telltale signs of past difficulties probably cause you to churn inside. After Naomi died, the Lord blessed us with two more children: Benj and Abby. Always strong and healthy, I never worried much about our son. However, Abby suffered with health problems during the first few years of her life.

On one occasion, I felt like I was back in the nightmare of Naomi's death. After being unwell for a few days, Abby suddenly went downhill fast. Soon we were at the hospital while doctors tried to identify the cause of her listlessness. God came through and healed our precious princess, but I was shattered by the experience. Over the next week or two, I was subdued and felt numb. Although I was healed of the pain of losing Naomi, I was still afraid of the thought of suffering such a trauma again. I got on my knees and gave God every memory of the trauma of Naomi's sudden death, then I gave Him every fear of facing grief again. I declared the words of 1 Corinthians 15:55: "O Death, where is your sting? O Hades, where is your victory?" A weight lifted off my heart. I then dedicated my children to Him afresh. Never again was I gripped with the fear of their death.

Do you worry that you will encounter a similar crisis again? Perhaps tell-tale signs of friction in your marriage make you afraid that you will experience the devastation of divorce all over again. Maybe when people are distant, you worry that you will go through another agonizing relationship breakdown. You could get nervous of another betrayal when you see leaders taking time out. Sickness may cause undue anxiety, or it could be something completely different that makes you uneasy. Whatever it is, the Lord does not want you to be afraid of pain or crisis. He wants your heart to be at peace.

We have covered several of the enemy's plots to keep you stuck in pain. Let's bring each one to the Lord in prayer. I suggest that you pray about each one even if you don't think they all apply to you. Sometimes, heart issues are hidden, but as we pray, a burden lifts that we did not even know was weighing us down. Let's pray.

Heavenly Father,

I come to You with an open heart. Lord, I have been through some difficult experiences and now realize that the enemy has been using buried pain to keep me bound. I have settled in the valley of the shadow of death, but I am now ready to leave its darkness and sadness. (*Now tell the Lord about any tragedy or crisis that He brought to your remembrance. Tell Him what happened and how it made you feel, share in as much detail as possible.*) I ask You to heal every hidden hurt, I will no longer ignore sadness, I will bring it to You. I am ready to experience Your joy again.

I realize that in the midst of crisis, I made some negative declarations. Today I choose to break the power of those words. (*Now tell the Lord anything you have said. Perhaps, like me, you suggested your situation was the worst? Maybe you announced that you would never recover. You could have said that would always be affected by the calamity. Tell God what you declared.*) Lord, I ask for Your forgiveness for making destructive declarations. In the name of Jesus, I break the power of those words now. I will not believe the enemy's lies anymore. Thank You that I can be completely healed because of the price that Jesus paid on the Cross. I expect to come out the other side.

Lord, I am sorry for blaming people for my pain. I realize now that blame is futile and only holds me in anger. I choose to let go of the things that people did that hurt me. I let go of the things they did not do that could have helped me. I let go of any mistakes that were made, I lay them down. I do not need someone to hold responsible, I only want to be free. (*Now tell the Lord about anyone you blamed. Tell Him that you lay it down today and forever.*) I will no longer waste my energy blaming, instead I ask You to heal my heart and restore my life.

I have suffered Lord, but today I make an important decision. I lay down all the questions that are trapping me in torment. I don't know why these things happened (*now tell the Lord exactly what you have struggled to accept, tell Him about any bewilderment*). I realize that my questions have been keeping me in confusion. So today, I give up my right to an answer, I lay down why, I give You every sense of injustice. I lay it all down at Your feet. Instead of an answer, Lord, I ask You to heal my heart.

The enemy tempted me to believe some horrible lies, Lord. I thought you were my problem God. I held You responsible for my suffering, but I now know I was wrong. You are the only One who can really help, You are a good, good Father and You have a plan to bring me through every difficulty. Jesus, thank You for caring so much that You died for me, thank You that You have never left me, and You will always be with me. I am so grateful that You care about every detail of my life. I realize how much my pain pained You. Thank You for loving me, I ask You to heal my heart.

Since experiencing certain traumas, I have been afraid of experiencing similar pain again. I give You every worry, every fear and all anxiety. Thank You that my life is in Your hands. I ask You to heal any trauma associated with the past, reveal anything that makes me wary and restore me, I pray. I refuse to be afraid of going through the same again. The past is gone!

Thank You for revealing these barriers to my healing, I ask You to heal me from the inside out so that I can embrace the life You died to provide.

In Jesus name I pray,

Amen.

Chapter 9

GOD'S PURPOSE

God has phenomenal plans for your life. What the enemy meant for your harm, the Lord wants to turn around for your good and the wellbeing of others. He wants to lead you into a bright future (see Jeremiah 29:11) and bring you to rich fulfillment. In this final chapter, we are going to look at the journey back to joy after crisis. Proverbs 4:23 (TPT) says, "So above all, guard the affections of your heart, for they affect all that you are. Pay attention to the welfare of your innermost being, for from there flows the wellspring of life."

Your heart is unique. Just as no two people are really identical, no one else has a heart like yours. Psalms 33:15 says, "He fashions their hearts individually..." There may be times when you feel like no one understands what you have been through. That's true: they could not know how you're feeling because they aren't you. The only One who knows exactly what is going on inside is the Lord. He knows every secret of your heart (see Psalms 44:21b). Even when you aren't sure why you feel a certain way, He knows. John 2:25 (NLT) says, "... He knew what was in each person's heart." God, who knows you, wants to bring total restoration to your soul, and therefore your life.

Structural Healing

I don't know which memories still cause you to react, but God knows. Maybe it is a betrayal or the breakdown of your marriage.

It could be a tragic loss or an awful accident. You may be doing better most of the time, or you could still be broken-hearted. Wherever you are at on your journey, God wants you to bring every source of pain to Him in prayer. Each time you come into His presence, tell Him what is hurting at that moment. Talk to Him as your Wonderful Counsellor (see Isaiah 9:6). After you have shared your heart, ask the Lord to refill your soul with His precious healing love.

Perhaps you are well on your way to recovery, but certain things still sting. Lamentations 3:20 says, "My soul still remembers and sinks within me." What still causes your heart to sink? Your inner churnings are indicators of unhealed hurts. Any memory that still causes sadness is a memory that your Heavenly Father wants to restore. He does not want to leave any wound untreated. Jesus wants to heal you anywhere you hurt.

Pain does not disappear if it is ignored. It may be buried, but it will eventually surface. This usually happens under the spotlight of your closest relationships. Left untreated, pain won't go. However, it might grow. Psalms 25:17 says, "The troubles of my heart have enlarged; bring me out of my distresses!" If you leave a bodily wound untreated, it can get infected and become a bigger problem. Emotional hurts are the same. Ignoring pain can make it worse.

If you're not sure what is wrong, but you know you're not completely free, invite the Holy Spirit to uncover hidden hurts. Proverbs 20:27 says, "The spirit of a man is the lamp of the Lord, searching all the inner depths of his heart." Spend time in prayer with an open heart. Ask God to shine His light into every corner of your heart and reveal unresolved issues. Don't turn away from any pain He reveals. Instead, face it while you are in His presence, then share your memories and feelings with the Lord. Tell Him how they affected you. As you talk to the Lord, trapped words will be released.

The Lord is watching over you, giving you the loving care that you need to bring you back to full health. Psalms 147:3 says,

"He heals the brokenhearted and binds up their wounds." *Raphah*, the Hebrew for heals, is the same word that is used elsewhere in the Bible for curing physical pain. Just as the Lord wants to mend a broken arm, so He is committed to healing your broken heart. This verse goes a step further. Your Heavenly Father wants to bind up and take care of your wounds.

A Precious Intimacy

Think about one of your close friends. I am sure that you have shared things with them that you have not told mere acquaintances. When you talk about your personal life and let someone see the real you, you develop a meaningful bond. In the light of that principle, let's look at Lamentations 2:19b: "Pour out your heart like water before the face of the Lord…" There are two outcomes when you share your heart with the Lord. You release pent up emotion resulting in tremendous relief. But that's not all, you develop a lasting intimacy with your Heavenly Father. The pain leaves and you grow closer than ever to Jesus, but there is more…

God reveals two ways that He restores in Psalms 147:3: "He heals the brokenhearted and binds up their wounds." He heals, but He also binds up wounds. I already shared the meaning in Hebrew for heal – it means to cure or repair. Your Heavenly Father is ready to cure all your inner turmoil! The second word for healing in this verse is very precious. Hâbaš means to bind up or bandage a wound.

Imagine a child who badly scraped his knee running into the arms of his loving mother. Now picture that mom gently cleaning the cut while comforting her little boy. Once clean, she would apply a soothing ointment, then protect her son's sensitive skin with a soft sticky plaster. Not only would this little boy's knee be made better, but he would feel the comfort and love of his mother. This is a picture of God's hâbaš healing. Your Heavenly Father wants you to experience His closeness while He heals your heart, He wants you to feel the tenderness of His love. When you have encountered

His ḥâbaš healing, you are restored, *and* you develop a closer relationship with the Lord. What a priceless gift!

Words Of Life

Hebrews 11:3 says, "By faith we understand that the worlds were framed by the word of God, so that the things which are seen were not made of things which are visible." God framed the world with His words. I will repeat something I shared in chapter 8… Looking at my husband just days after Naomi died, I said, "My love, this will not destroy us." Looking back, I believe that my declaration helped frame our story. Even at the outset, we had a hope that we would come out the other side intact. In the aftermath of any disaster, you can use your mouth to pave the way out of the wilderness. In the last chapter, we broke the power of negative words. Now we are going to look at the strength you can obtain by speaking words of life. You can use your tongue to breathe hope and life into your soul.

We are made in the image of God, and that's what He did at the start of time. Genesis 1:2-3 (AMP) says, "The earth was without form and an empty waste, and darkness was upon the face of the very great deep. The Spirit of God was moving (hovering, brooding) over the face of the waters. And God said, Let there be light; and there was light." With emptiness and darkness all around, God declared light. As well as speaking the Word of God in my prayer times, before I thank God for my breakfast in a morning, I always declare out loud, "This is the day the Lord has made, I will rejoice and be glad in it!" (Psalm 118:24). I am using my words to frame my day. You can do the same.

Paul's Perspective

The best way to greet a crisis is to be well prepared. A friend once explained why he retired to the East Coast of America instead of the West Coast: "You get warnings about hurricanes," he told me, "but you don't get warnings about earthquakes." His 40 years working for the fire department had made him calamity-conscious in a way that affected almost every area of his life.

Psalms 112:1-10 (NASB) is a manual for Christian living, but it also provides a crisis preparation system. It reads, "Praise the LORD! How blessed is the man who fears the LORD, Who greatly delights in His commandments. His descendants will be mighty on earth; The generation of the upright will be blessed. Wealth and riches are in his house, And his righteousness endures forever. Light arises in the darkness for the upright; He is gracious and compassionate and righteous. It is well with the man who is gracious and lends; He will maintain his cause in judgment. For he will never be shaken; The righteous will be remembered forever. He will not fear evil tidings; His heart is steadfast, trusting in the LORD. His heart is upheld, he will not fear, Until he looks with satisfaction on his adversaries. He has given freely to the poor, His righteousness endures forever; His horn will be exalted in honor. The wicked will see it and be vexed, He will gnash his teeth and melt away; The desire of the wicked will perish."

As well as being a template for how born-again believers should live, Psalm 112 provides a series of instructions for how we should confront Life's ABC's. I see these instructions as a check list. Adopting these principles ahead of a crisis is like having a hurricane pre-warning system at the ready. When the winds, rains, and floods strike, you are prepared. Jesus promised us that life's ABC's would find us at some stage, as sure as hurricanes happen in tropical areas. Matthew 7:24-25 is clear that the wise (as well as the foolish) will go through the storms of life: "Therefore whoever hears these sayings of Mine, and does them, I will liken him to a wise man who built his house on the rock: and the rain descended, the floods came, and the winds blew and beat on that house; and it did not fall, for it was founded on the rock." So how can we prepare?

No Fear

Psalm 112:7 (NASB) shows us the posture we need to adopt when crisis hits: "He will not fear evil tidings; His heart is steadfast, trusting in the LORD." This verse indicates that we must refuse to be afraid when we hear bad news. My wife puts it like this: "Fear is a controllable reflex." When bad news is announced or terrible things happen, we need to choose to respond, not react. We must refuse fear and keep our hearts focused on God.

Confidence In The Lord

Psalm 112:7 goes on to teach us to be calm and confident in the Lord even when shaking comes. The heart of one who trusts God remains steadfast. It cannot be easily moved or troubled even in the face of trauma. We can prepare by learning to calm our hearts. Practice quietening your heart when small things happen. When you can maintain your cool during minor difficulties, you will be better equipped to remain steadfast when big storms descend.

Endurance

One way to prepare spiritually, emotionally and mentally is to develop a warrior mindset. 2 Timothy 2:3 says, "You therefore must endure hardship as a good soldier of Jesus Christ." Seeing calamity as something we must all endure helps us resist panic and self-pity. I like to paraphrase this verse this way: "Suck it up soldier!" These are great scriptures to go back to any time the ABC's rear their heads.

Expect Accusation

If you're in any kind of leadership, people may judge you when the storms of life come your way: 'He must have done something terrible to deserve this', 'It's judgement!', 'This is the wages of sin.' It is important to resolve ahead of time that 'people will be people' in their quest for understanding your plight. It's almost always those who should know better who come out with the dumbest of reactions. During a recent health scare, instead of recognizing that we are all in a spiritual war (see Ephesians 6:10) and that the enemy sometimes tries to rob us of our health, a friend tried to convince me that my plight was a curse because I had been too bold in my preaching. Thankfully, I was already aware how fickle public opinion can be when observing things outwardly without understanding or having a revelation on the situation. If allegations come, we need to hold up the shield of faith, knock the enemy's arrows to the ground, and stay strong.

Dismiss Public Opinion

Acts 28:2-6 describes what happened when Paul was shipwrecked on the island of Malta: "And the natives showed us unusual kindness; for they kindled a fire and made us all welcome, because of the rain that was falling and because of the cold. But when Paul had gathered a bundle of sticks and laid them on the fire, a viper came out because of the heat, and fastened on his hand. So when the natives saw the creature hanging from his hand, they said to one another, "No doubt this man is a murderer, whom, though he has escaped the sea, yet justice does not allow to live." But he shook off the creature into the fire and suffered no harm. However, they were expecting that he would swell up or suddenly fall down dead. But after they had looked for a long time and saw no harm come to him, they changed their minds and said that he was a god."

The Apostle and his shipmates had been caught in rough seas for days, so Paul decided to help build a fire when they reached land. Whilst gathering sticks, a deadly snake bit the apostle. The locals jumped to the conclusion that the snake bit Paul because he was some kind of serial killer! Imagine the scene as the minutes ticked by and Paul was unharmed by the deadly venom, the apostle went from being a murderer in their eyes to a god. That's public opinion for you. If you have been judged in the middle of a storm, please know that you are not alone. Let the reactions and opinions of the people wash off you like water off a duck's back. Paul rebuked the church at Corinth for this kind of behavior (see 2 Corinthians 10:7). We must never engage in it, and if we see someone in trouble, even if they are a supposed 'enemy', we must try to help out. We may even be able to win them over (see Romans 12:20).

Daily Declarations

Earlier on in this chapter, Jo mentioned that she makes a declaration every day before she has her breakfast. I start my day with a whole series of declarations. I claim the blood of Jesus over myself and my loved ones, over our plans, our relationships, and our possessions. I declare that no weapon formed against us will prosper and that every tongue that rises up in judgement against us shall be condemned for our sakes. "This is the heritage of the servants of the Lord and their vindication is from me, says God." (Isaiah 54:17). I continue, "The Lord will send his angel ahead of us to prosper our way" (Genesis 24:40). Then I declare, "Wisdom, you are my sister, understanding, you are my close intimate friend." (Proverbs 7:4). I speak out: "Goodness and mercy shall follow us all the days of our lives, and we shall dwell in the house of the Lord forever." (Psalm 23:6). I do not stop there! "With long life you will satisfy us and fullness of days, we shall behold your salvation." (Psalm 91:16)

Making these faith filled statements daily saturates my day, my week, my year, and my entire life with the Word of God and heaven's resources. When I go through tough times, I know they are not the will of God, I understand that they are simply a season for me to pass through. When you get a moment, if you don't yet have a personal daily declaration, let me encourage you to draft one with the leadership and guidance of the Holy Spirit. It's one of the most life transforming things you can do. It's the equivalent of hurricane proofing your home.

I Forgave You Before I Met You

One key to enjoying lightness in your heart is to make sure you have a mechanism for dealing with life's junk quickly. The great faith and healing teacher, Kenneth Hagin, described it as keeping a short account with God. The Bible story of a man who owed the equivalent of US$3 billion, who was forgiven by his lender, only to beat and torment somebody for a debt of just a few hundred dollars, is a stark reminder from Jesus about how He values forgiveness. The Lord put a colossal monetary value on the debt of sin which we all owe to our Heavenly Father. The small debt was the wrongdoing of a fellow man.

Let's look at a story Jesus told in Matthew 18:23-35 (NLT): "Therefore, the Kingdom of Heaven can be compared to a king who decided to bring his accounts up to date with servants who had borrowed money from him. In the process, one of his debtors was brought in who owed him millions of dollars. He couldn't pay, so his master ordered that he be sold—along with his wife, his children, and everything he owned—to pay the debt. "But the man fell down before his master and begged him, 'Please, be patient with me, and I will pay it all.' Then his master was filled with pity for him, and he released him and forgave his debt. "But when the man left the king, he went to a fellow servant who owed him a few thousand dollars. He grabbed him by the throat and demanded instant payment.

"His fellow servant fell down before him and begged for a little more time. 'Be patient with me, and I will pay it,' he pleaded. But his creditor wouldn't wait. He had the man arrested and put in prison until the debt could be paid in full. "When some of the other servants saw this, they were very upset. They went to the king and told him everything that had happened. Then the king called in the man he had forgiven and said, 'You evil servant! I forgave you that tremendous debt because you pleaded with me. Shouldn't you have mercy on your fellow servant, just as I had mercy on you?' Then the angry king sent the man to prison to be

tortured until he had paid his entire debt. "That's what my heavenly Father will do to you if you refuse to forgive your brothers and sisters from your heart."

The story ends with the unforgiving servant being handed over to torturers, until the $3 billion debt was paid. That's probably a lot of torture! During a spiritual attack on the integrity of our ministry, the person spearheading the accusations momentarily apologized for what they had done. "Don't worry," I replied without thinking, "I forgave you before I met you." God gave me a word from Heaven in the middle of a storm and I knew that it must guide me from that day forward when it comes to forgiveness.

If you make a decision to let offenses go before they even happen, it will make it much easier when you need to release someone from a debt they owe. Decide right now that you are a quick forgiver and then declare it boldly. Sometimes the initial shock of an attack or a betrayal can knock you sideways, but that doesn't mean that you should stay down or deviate from your decision to live your life as a forgiver. Why not practice on one or two people? Tell them that you forgave them before you met them, and that you will never hold an offense against them. See what they say.

The Gift Of Surrender

When something awful has happened, it often leaves us with a terrible sense of injustice. Your loved one should never have had to suffer. That partner should not have destroyed your business. That leader should not have trashed your ministry. That family member should not have gone so soon. Your spouse should not have treated you so badly. Knowing that something was very wrong can make us feel like we must hang on to our hurts. If we let go, it may seem as though what happened was acceptable. Holding on seems right because what happened was wrong. In truth, this is a cruel lie whispered by the enemy into the ears of a hurting person.

Proverbs 14:12 explains, "There is a way that seems right to a man, but its end is the way of death." Clinging to the upset only keeps you bound to pain. While you hang onto the injustice, you are also holding on to the hurt. This traps you in the past. It's a difficult place. Although surrendering seems hard at the start, it leads to great relief. When we let go of the wrong, we walk out of an invisible prison and into a place where we can be restored.

Sometimes we must surrender the injustice, other times we must let go of the pain and occasionally, we need to lay down our regrets. After Ben died at the tender age of eight, Kate was burdened by many regrets. She agonized over what she could have done better, she wished she had spent more time just holding her son and appreciating him. Kate felt bad for feeling so tired and overwhelmed while he was sick. In short, she longed to turn back the clock and do things differently.

At our two-day conference Healed for Life, I spoke about regret and guilt. During this session, Kate realized that she could not change the past, but now understood she could trust God for her future. This precious mom made a monumental decision: she handed all her regrets and her 'if only's' to the Lord as an offering. Almost immediately she felt a release; a heavy weight of grief lifted, and a deep sadness evaporated. Kate never again was weighed down by regret.

The Right Way To Cry

There is a big difference between a few tears and pouring out pain. In Psalm 18:6, David said, "I cried out to You in my distress... and... You heard my troubled cry. My sobs came right into Your heart and You turned Your face to rescue me." (TPT). Crying *out* is not the same as crying. When we cry out, there is a thrust behind our tears and agony leaves. Crying is simply tears falling. After trauma, there is usually a reservoir of pain trapped inside. It needs to be released. David knew how to let go in God's presence. In Psalms 6:6 (NLT), he said, "I am worn out from sobbing.

All night I flood my bed with weeping, drenching it with my tears." When you have suffered a great deal, you need to pour out your pain in prayer.

Another important point is that crying bitter tears is not the same as surrendering your pain in God's presence. Bitter tears are rooted in a sense of injustice, and are usually full of frustration. They demand an explanation. When we come into the presence of the Lord, we must be willing to let go of our sorrow. After the instruction to "...Pour out your heart like water before the face of the Lord." Lamentations 2:19b continues, "Lift your hands toward Him..." Lifting your hands is a universal sign of surrender. While you want to hold onto your right to be hurt, it will be difficult to be healed. When you surrender every ounce of pain in the presence of the Lord, He will bring lasting restoration.

The Joy Of Trust

Earlier in this book, we talked about the importance of placing our trust in God again and again, especially after betrayal. It is also important that we intentionally put our trust back in the Lord after going through a crisis or a shaking. Calamity is shocking. It can change your view of the world and of people. It can even shake your faith. The enemy wants you to withdraw your trust from God. He wants you to become wary and suspicious. But if I don't trust God, I am putting my trust in myself instead. Proverbs 28:26 explains the danger: "He who trusts in his own heart is a fool, but whoever walks wisely will be delivered." It is always wise to trust God, especially if you have been through any kind of tragedy.

Trust, by definition, involves taking a step into the unknown. It is saying, 'I may have been through a battering, but I'm not going to build walls around my heart. I choose to trust God again.' King David often declared in the psalms something along the lines of: "I put my trust in You" (see, for example, Psalm 56:11). In Psalms 25:1-2 (AMP) he declared: "Unto You, O Lord, do I bring my life. O my God, I trust, lean on, rely on, and am confident in You..."

If your trust has crumbled, I encourage you today to put your trust back in God. If you still trust, but you have been shaken, again, I invite you to place all your confidence in Him. He will never leave you nor forsake you.

The Turn Around

Our awesome God is not just a Master Restorer, He also has the power to bring good out of even our most painful seasons. I already shared that this precious ministry was birthed out of the death of our dear daughter. God took the enemy's plan to destroy our family and turned it into a source of life for many. There are countless Biblical examples of the Lord turning problems into platforms for His purposes. Sarah's old, barren womb became the birthplace of the nation of Israel. God used a painful betrayal as Joseph's transport system from Canaan to Egypt where his destiny would be fulfilled.

The Lord transformed a man with a filthy mouth into the mouthpiece of God. Isaiah 6:5 (NLT) records the prophet's words: "It's all over! I am doomed, for I am a sinful man. I have filthy lips, and I live among a people with filthy lips. Yet I have seen the King, the Lord of Heaven's Armies." After losing every member of her nuclear family and writing herself off, Naomi went on to become the great, great grandmother of King David who is named in the lineage of Jesus Christ (see Matthew 1:5).

The verse that I am about to share is not only true when you are overlooked for a promotion or lose a contract, but also in every season of your life. Romans 8:28 (NASB) states: "And we know that God causes all things to work together for good to those who love God, to those who are called according to His purpose." The first three words: "And we know..." emphasize the infallibility of this truth. When you and I love God enough to place our entire lives into His hands, He will turn even trauma and tragedy around for good. I encourage you to give every detail of your life to God.

Make a decision that it is no longer your calamity, but now you give it to your Heavenly Father to turn for good.

A Unique Opportunity

Before the first anniversary of Naomi's death, God graciously blessed my husband and me with a lovely baby boy, Benjy. When our son was eighteen months, I went into labor with our third child. Everything was going well until the baby's head emerged. "Stop pushing!" the midwife yelled as she called for help. Soon the birthing room was filled with medics. "Your umbilical cord is wrapped twice around your baby's neck," A doctor explained, "Each push was strangling your little one. We need to cut the cord and get your child out now." In a flash, the baby was out, and the team of doctors left for the neonatal emergency room. "Go with the baby," I called to my husband. Soon I was alone with one midwife.

About thirty minutes after the emergency team left the room, I discovered that I had given birth to a little girl. With kindness in her voice, the nurse explained, "The doctors are doing everything they can, but we still don't know if your baby will survive." To be honest, I was so dazed by the shock that her words glazed over me. Soon the midwife moved me from the birthing unit to a treatment room. It was while they were patching me up that reality hit like a punch in the guts. "What is it with me and girls?" I cried out to the Lord. After crying out to the Lord, I spoke to God again: "I don't know how this story will end, Lord, but I promise You this: whether she lives or dies, I will win people to Jesus as vengeance. And I will pray more."

We have a unique opportunity in the middle of a crisis to show the Lord how much we love Him. Exhausted and empty, I had no faith in that moment. (Thankfully, my husband was praying for her life.) Yes, I could have bargained. But He is God, and I am His creation. Instead of trying to bribe God, I told Him that my love and loyalty had no conditions. Looking back, I am grateful for the opportunity.

In the place of uncertainty, we get the chance to imitate three Hebrew men before they were hurled into a huge furnace. Addressing the king who ordered that they be burned, the men said: "...the God we serve is able to deliver us from it, and he will deliver us from Your Majesty's hand. But even if he does not, we want you to know, Your Majesty, that we will not serve your gods or worship the image of gold you have set up." (Daniel 3:17-18 NIV). These men were clear, whatever the outcome, we are serving God.

The Journey

One of the most common questions I am asked about the heart is this: "How do I know if I am really healed?" There are two answers, both are equally important. Firstly, you know you are whole by examining the evidence. Let me explain... If you had been badly bruised in an accident, you would know that you were healed when your body no longer hurt, even if someone banged the affected areas. We know that the Lord has restored our souls when pointed reminders don't cause pain. We know we have recovered when we can look back at memories with peace and joy. (The joy comes from the realization that you are healed!)

There is a second answer. Psalms 64:6b says, "Both the inward thought and the heart of man are deep." The human soul is vast and complex. Our hearts have hidden chambers or caves (see Proverbs 20:27). I have no doubt that it's in those secret places of the soul that pain gets buried, and issues hidden. We think we know ourselves, but more often than not, we don't have a clue what is going on deep inside. Jeremiah 17:9 (AMP) explains: "The heart is deceitful above all things... Who can know it [perceive, understand, be acquainted with his own heart and mind]?" The person your heart is most likely to lie to is you. The truth can be painful, so your heart will tell you all is well when that is not the case. So, instead of assuming that you are healed, and that God is finished, keep your heart open and stay on your healing journey until you step into the joy of eternity. Let's pray.

Heavenly Father,

I am so grateful for what You have done in me as I have read this book. But I want more, Lord. I don't want to tolerate any buried pain, I want to live my whole life to please You, so I know my heart has to be whole. I ask You to reveal any wounds still affecting my soul as a result of painful seasons. I won't turn away from uncomfortable memories any more Lord. (*Now talk to the Lord about any thoughts or experiences that He has brought to your remembrance while you have been reading. Tell Him what you went through and how it all made you feel. Share in as much detail as you can.*) I bring You my pain Lord and I ask You to take it away. I surrender all my sadness and I give You every sense of injustice. I give You every tragedy or calamity that wounded me. I place all these experiences in Your hands.

Now I ask You to pour Your wonderful healing love into the depths of my soul. I receive Your precious healing balm. I receive Your love deep down. Thank You for filling every empty place in my soul with Your precious Spirit. I am Yours Lord, and You are mine. My life is in Your hands. Where my world was shaken, I put my trust in You again. I give You complete control of my life.

I ask You Lord to take every trauma and tragedy that I have endured and turn each one for good. Take my pain and use it for Your purpose. Take what the enemy meant for harm and use it for my good and for the good of many others too. Have Your way in my heart and be glorified in my life. I declare that good will come out of every difficult moment.

My life and my future are in Your hands, and I will fulfill all my God-given destiny.

In Jesus' name I pray,

Amen.

What's Next?

Your heart is probably your most valuable, and yet your most vulnerable, asset. This book is just part of your journey to healing and freedom. As you finish this book, make the decision to continue to prioritize your inner wellbeing. Visit JoNaughton.com to find out about our resources to help you to wholeness. The Heart Academy provides life-changing courses by Zoom on topics like Breaking The Power Of Rejection, Healing Inevitable Marriage Hurts, and Overcoming Insecurity. We have a mentoring network, online courses, and a range of print, digital, and audio books. We run half day, full day, and two-day events for adults and children, all designed to help you on your journey. Above all, look after your heart every day of your life, for it determines the course of your life.

"I am convinced and sure of this very thing, that He who began a good work in you will continue until the day of Jesus Christ (right up to the time of His return), developing [that good work] and perfecting and bringing it to full completion in you." (Philippians 1:6 AMP)

Let that word sink deep into you. God is preparing you for your destiny. He has already started the job, and He will be faithful to finish it.

An Invitation

If you would like to ask Jesus to become the Lord of your life, I would be honored to lead you in a simple prayer. The Bible says that God loves you and that Jesus wants to draw close to you: "Behold I stand at the door and knock. If anyone hears My voice and opens the door, I will come in." (Revelation 3:20) If you would like to know Jesus as your Friend, your Savior, and your Lord, the first step is to ask. Pray this prayer:

Dear Lord,

I know that You love me and have a wonderful plan for my life. I ask You to come into my heart today and be my Savior and Lord. Forgive me for all my sins, I pray. Thank You that because You died on the cross for me, I am forgiven of every wrong I have ever committed when I repent. I give my life to You entirely and ask You to lead me in Your ways from now on.

In Jesus' name,

Amen.

If you have prayed this prayer for the first time, it will be important to tell a Christian friend what you prayed and to find a good church. Just as a newborn baby needs nourishment and care, so you (and all Christians) need the support of other believers as you start your new life as a follower of Jesus Christ.

You can watch free Bible messages that will help to build your faith by subscribing to Jo Naughton's YouTube channel and to Harvest Church London's YouTube channel. You can follow Paul and Jo on Instagram (@paulnaughton_, @jonaughton_), and go on Facebook and like our public pages (Paul Naughton, Jo Naughton). God bless you!

About The Authors

Paul Naughton followed the call of God into full-time ministry after a successful career in banking. He has preached in major crusades, at conferences, and in churches in 28 nations across four continents. Paul has great authority in the Word and moves under a strong prophetic anointing, bringing the supernatural power of God with signs following. He has been featured on television and radio networks across Europe, Africa, and the Americas.

Paul is the Founder and Senior Pastor of Harvest Church in London, England, which he leads together with Jo. He is also Executive Director of Whole Heart Ministries founded by his wife, Jo. Paul is passionate about raising up mighty prayer warriors in the UK.

You can connect with Paul via
www.harvestchurch.org.uk
YouTube Harvest Church London
Instagram @paulnaughton_

Jo Naughton is the founder of Whole Heart Ministries, which is dedicated to helping people be free to fulfill their God-given purpose. Together with Paul, Jo pastors Harvest Church in London, England. A public relations executive turned pastor, Jo's previous career included working for King Charles (while he was the Prince) as an executive VP of his largest charity. After reaching the pinnacle of the public relations world, Jo felt the call of God to full-time ministry. She is a regular guest on TV and radio shows in the US and UK.

An international speaker and author, Jo ministers with a heart-piercing anointing, sharing with great personal honesty in conferences and at churches around the world. Her passion is to see people set free from all inner hindrances so that they can fulfill their God-given destiny. Countless people have testified to having received powerful and life-changing healing through her ministry. Paul and Jo have two wonderful children, Ben and Abby.

You can connect with Jo via:
JoNaughton.com
Instagram @jonaughton_
YouTube Jo Naughton
Facebook public page – Jo Naughton

Also By The Author:

All of Paul and Jo Naughton's books are available at: JoNaughton.com

www.ingramcontent.com/pod-product-compliance
Lightning Source LLC
Chambersburg PA
CBHW020805160426
43192CB00006B/443